The Door Whore

Confessions of a Restaurant Diva

A Novel by
Fern Esposito

Little Print Press

For further information please go to www.thedoorwhore.net

Cover design by Shawn Esposito, shawn@rendertank.com

Printed in the United States of America

The Door Whore: Confessions of a Restaurant Diva
Fern Esposito

1. Title 2. Author 3. Fiction

LCCN: 2007907045

ISBN 10: 0-9799843-0-0
ISBN 13: 978-0-9799843-0-3

To Peter

Table of Contents

Chapter 1

The Adventure Begins

My name is Ivy Zingara, I am the door whore, and this is my story.

A "door whore" is not actually a whore as one would commonly think of the term. In restaurant lingo, it is a derogatory term describing the female who greets you upon entering a fine dining establishment. Of course, most diners would probably view that person as a hostess. If you have ever been employed in a restaurant, you may have heard the expression "door whore"—or perhaps the term "the bitch up front" may be the more common title. Whatever the case, that was me for five years.

Please bear in mind that I was not your run-of-the-mill door whore. *Au contraire*, I was the ultimate door whore! I owned the establishment. I created it, named it, designed it; controlled the reservation book; hired, fired and trained the staff; and battled with the kitchen whenever necessary.

I named my creation "Sentimento" and diligently worked to make it fabulous. It was a dream come true for me and I was more than willing to work the eighty to one hundred hours a week to keep it running efficiently. I have often felt that in many ways, owning a restaurant is much like having a naughty child that demands your constant attention. And like the ocean, you should never turn your back on it.

I maintained my position at the podium regardless of exhaustion, illness or injury for five tumultuous years, as I experienced the quintessential emotional roller coaster ride of a lifetime.

The restaurant business is truly a twenty-four/seven operation—at least, if you plan to do it correctly. You must be present all the time and every day, because without fail, there is always a *crisis du jour*! This may range from something as innocuous as only receiving half your linen order to the more serious problem of running out of fish on Good Friday. Oh yes, and then there's always the potential of something disastrous happening, such as a waiter or chef being incarcerated in New York City on a Friday or Saturday and requesting bail money from you.

The most common *crisis du jour* usually involves either an employee showing up drunk for work, or a bloody fistfight between a cook and a waiter during the dinner rush. Your life is never boring. There is constant drama, keeping the atmosphere surrounding you electrified and fascinating at all times.

It's hard for me to know exactly how to begin the story of my odyssey, but I will do my best to relay each important chaotic detail. First, I would like to emphatically state that I possessed no background in the restaurant business whatsoever, nor did my husband, Vincent. He is an extremely successful venture capitalist. I had a nursing background but eventually switched to medical sales and went to work for a large pharmaceutical company.

My professional title of clinical sales specialist was imprinted on my business cards, but in reality it just sounded more impressive than "detail person." My job involved calling on physicians and hospitals and doing my best to convince anyone who would listen why my products were far superior to any other company's. I plied nurses and receptionists with mugs adorned with my company logo and bumper stickers that read, "Love a Nurse PRN," along with an assortment of freebies all geared toward gaining access to the inner sanctum of the DOCTOR'S PRIVATE OFFICE. Upon entering their *sanctum sanctorum,* I would do my best to give the physician my shtick about whatever products the company had instructed my division to promote that particular quarter.

While I was busy calling on physicians, my husband was busy creating successful businesses, buying up real estate and working ten to eighteen hours a day, six to seven days a week.

I was also successful at my job and continued until my daughter was seven months old. I had worked until my due date—she was ten days late—and after all, who wouldn't give an obviously very pregnant woman the sale? I waddled my way through my territory, smiling as I stacked up sale after sale. It was great being number one in my division! My pregnancy was the most effective sales aid I possessed; it certainly surpassed all those bumper stickers.

When my daughter was three months old, I returned to work slimmed down and armed with pictures of THE BABY.

Upon retiring from my position as a detail person extraordinaire, I worked with my husband, helping him build his little empire. When word spread that I was opening my own restaurant, all the local papers did feature stories on the soon to be opened Sentimento.

I am not Italian. I am of Hungarian descent, and when customers would ask me what part of Italy "my people" were from, I would smile and say, "Budapest." However, my husband is very Italian. Vincent—a.k.a. Vin, Vince, Vinnie or Zingo; he will answer to any variation of his name—practically has the map of Italy on his handsome face. He has olive skin, black hair and dark brown, "gypsy" eyes. I am near the opposite end of the color spectrum and often appear as though I could use a transfusion. I inherited my father's fair skin, reddish hair and blue eyes. We're a match made if not in heaven, then in New Jersey.

So how did the restaurant come about? you may ask. The answer is simple, complex and naïve. Please note that I neglected to include the words "stupid" or "obtuse," which of course was what I was when it came to the restaurant business.

A chef we knew for several years, and whose cooking we loved, came over for coffee one night. The next day, I was out looking for the perfect location and thinking of the perfect name to call it. There you had it: my dream of owning an Italian restaurant had finally come true and Sentimento was conceived. I must admit that it was a slightly capricious beginning.

Now wait, this bit of information is probably important: Vincent and I are workaholics. The work ethic had been drilled into both of us as we grew up and neither hard work nor long hours frightened us. Meanwhile, as the close friends we confided in about our plans tried to convince us to seek professional psychiatric counseling immediately, we merely laughed it off...after all, we knew exactly what we were doing.

Coulda...woulda...shoulda...

Chapter 2

The Set-up

The search for the perfect location did not take long. It was on a main street in Summit, a gentrified and affluent town with a very strong shopping area and walking traffic; it was considered very upscale and in my opinion would be the perfect locale for my dream restaurant.

There was only one problem: the location I desired

was in a building that was approximately a hundred years old and occupied by a dumpy luncheonette decorated in shades of purple, orange, black and chartreuse—not to mention completely falling apart, literally!

The building was owned by a group of investors with a Nazi mentality and a penchant for greed. Their monthly rental request was exorbitant and infeasible, as were the terms of the lease; I resumed my search.

Over the next eighteen months, I tried repeatedly to obtain this ideal location, each time failing miserably. If it wasn't the luncheonette owner demanding hundreds of thousands of dollars for his useless and nonexistent business, it was the landlords making unrealistic demands on the lease. I finally gave up on the location and started looking further south; that was when everyone and everything just came together.

In August 1998, we bought the luncheonette business in order to obtain the space and agreed on terms for the lease. Vincent and I cracked open a bottle of champagne and celebrated. What a couple of schmucks we were, totally clueless of the bullshit, grief and aggravation we were about to endure.

The first thing I did was apply for a demolition permit in order to gut the place. I thought it would take about ten minutes to obtain the permit since I had submitted plans completed by a local architect, who had assured me there would be no problems acquiring the permit. I had all my sub-contractors waiting in the wings to begin work.

Three weeks later, I finally received the permit. The sub-contractors I had hired had moved on to other jobs, and thus began a waiting game for the "subs" and inspections, praying for approvals and having to constantly rely on my husband to deal with the workmen, who didn't want to take any instructions from me. Some of them just ignored me while others did spiteful things in an attempt to aggravate and upset me. One worker seemed to knock off his jollies by defecating in all three of the brand new toilets and never flushing, while others enjoyed putting out their cigarettes on the newly laid ceramic tile floor despite the numerous "NO SMOKING" signs.

Inspectors refused to speak to me and only wanted to deal with my husband. One afternoon, one of the numerous inspectors, a total misogynist, stopped in while my architect, Benjamin, was there. Benjamin immediately went over to say hello and I followed him. I introduced myself to the inspector. I stood there next to the inspector while he pontificated on how we better do this and that. Then, I spoke up and respectfully stated, "Could you please give us all the requirements in writing so that we are able to comply with each and every regulation?"

He stared at me, then looked directly at Benjamin and snarled, "Tell her I don't put anything in writing." He stormed out in a huff.

After a few weeks of trying to combat this prejudice, I realized I was fighting a losing battle and changed tactics. Whenever the occasion arose, I just played the naïve and passive little wife who would check with her hubby, the "man of the house" who made all the decisions. This charade actually worked to my advantage for a while, but the problem was, it was hard to keep up the façade since I was neither a naïve nor passive individual.

We had planned to open before Thanksgiving 1998, which did not happen. We had been "grandfathered" in on certain expensive areas such as not requiring an extra ADA (American Disabilities Act) restroom; our kitchen ventilation system had also been inspected, approved and "grandfathered" in.

Unfortunately, two months into the project, we were informed it was necessary to add the ADA facility. We immediately had our architect redesign the space to comply with the new regulation changes. We also remodeled the entire kitchen in order to meet all the current code requirements.

In December, as we were waiting for our certificate of occupancy, I received a "stop work" notice from one of the fire inspectors. I was informed that the entire kitchen had to be ripped out, including the pre-approved ventilation system. Even the walls had to be replaced because of a new change in the code requirements, due to several grease fires that occurred the previous year at local restaurants.

Now, since I was using my own money to finance this project, to say I was distraught is an understatement. Vincent remained calm, cool and collected and we rolled up our sleeves not only figuratively but literally as well. We managed to hire additional people to do the labor and kitchen suppliers to customize the kitchen.

After an additional expense of about twenty thousand dollars, we had to just sit, wait and hope for our approvals. They finally came at the end of January 1999, and we were able to open at long last. We planned a "soft" opening the first week, just unlock and open the front door and see what happens, and that's exactly what we did.

The night before we officially opened to the public, we did a practice run. We invited friends and local dignitaries to be our guests for dinner.

So there I was in my exquisitely chic new restaurant, scared out of my mind yet trying my best to appear confident while standing at the hand-carved mahogany podium, in my brand new designer black suit. I didn't realize that I was about to embark on one of the most outrageous ventures of my life. The next few years would be a combination of the agony and the ecstasy. What you are about to read are little bits and pieces of my life as the ultimate door whore!

Chapter 3

The Staff

As I began to hire the dining room staff of servers, runners and bussers for our not-yet-opened restaurant, I think I was initially overly concerned with their appearances. Unfortunately, I actually believed the fraudulent statements they told regarding their expertise, varied abilities and experience.

It is almost virtually impossible to receive an accurate reference on a prospective employee in the restaurant business. Owners and managers are reluctant and fearful to tell you that so-and-so has a drug or drinking problem, or that someone is a thief or has a personality disorder. Everyone, and I mean everyone, is so fearful and skittish of being sued that they won't give you an honest reference. Due to this litigious situation, I really had to rely on my gut instinct and restaurant gossip to find out who should and should not be hired.

Reality quickly set in when three days before we opened, the fellow I had hired to be the head waiter overdosed and was admitted to a rehabilitation facility, never to be heard from again. By the third month we were open, I became somewhat more astute at assessing prospective employees, although out of desperation, I would have an occasional lapse in judgment, which I would quickly try to rectify—but that is another chapter in itself.

I had purchased solid amber shirts and matching solid amber ties for all the servers—very monochromatic. They were to be worn with black trousers and short, black aprons. The bussers and runners would wear black trousers and tan jackets. They all looked clean cut and very professional.

However, my initial choices in hiring left a lot to be desired. I was a total neophyte, and my dining room staff knew I was a novice and took full advantage of the situation.

One of the things I was unprepared for was the fact that the kitchen, known as the back of the house, and the dining room staff, known as the front of the house, always hate each other. I had no idea that this dynamic would cause me nightmares for years to come—not to mention numerous Zantac prescriptions and gallons of Mylanta to treat the agita, and numerous bottles of Advil to help combat the headaches this situation created.

There were many days I entered the restaurant feeling like a warden in an insane asylum, and just hoped and prayed I wouldn't become one of the inmates.

There also came a time when I employed so many alcoholics, recovering alcoholics and soon-to-become total alcoholics, I could have had AA meetings in the dining room of Sentimento. I actually contacted my lawyer at one point to check to see if I was within my rights to do random drug screening periodically; he advised against it.

I was also concerned about the correct and legal procedure to ask certain questions when interviewing and hiring prospective employees. I took a course in the legalities of all types of workplace harassment—sexual, ethnic and so on. Since I could not control my chefs' mouths and the vile statements that often spewed forth from them, I considered investing in an expensive insurance rider that covered this area.

The language articulated in the kitchen is difficult to describe. Let us just say that "motherfucker" was one of the more innocuous and innocent profanities used by my chefs. "Cock sucker" was usually a favorite on Saturday nights around eight-thirty or nine p.m., when the first "hissy fit" of the evening would occur.

My executive chef, Christopher, had regular tantrums during the week; however, he went totally psycho on weekends, holidays and during large, private parties. His behavior would then become tantamount to that of a deeply disturbed individual or a demonically possessed man. I just was never sure if I needed to call an exorcist or a ghostbuster, or perhaps locate a psychiatrist who would be willing to administer copious doses of Valium, Lithium Carbonate, Paxil or any anti-psychotic medication... STAT!

The following is a handy glossary of helpful restaurant terms and slang. It will be useful throughout the book, and will also be a benefit if you ever lose your mind and decide to open up a restaurant.

The Sentimento Guide
to Restaurant Slang

Door whore: The person who greets you upon entering a dining establishment. In my case, that would be me!

Server: Another term for waiter or waitress.

Station: Specific tables assigned to each server.

Back of the house: The kitchen staff.

Front of the house: Servers, busboys, runners, sommelier, maitre d' and me. Any employee of the dining room that has contact with the customers.

Amuse bouche: A French term for a small one- or two-bite-sized portion intended to tantalize a diner's taste buds. We referred to it as "the gift" and we sent one out to each table, at no cost to the customer, along with the bread.

Deuce: A dinner party consisting of two diners.

Four top: A table of four. (Five, six, seven and so on is referred to as the number of people in the dining party followed by the word top... five top, six top, etc.)

Fire: Cook it now!

86: Having run out of an item.

Walk a check: When a customer leaves without paying the bill.

Dupes: The kitchen's copies of the customers' food orders.

In the weeds: When the kitchen is jammed up and running behind on dinner orders.

Slammed: A night, or part of a night, spent "in the weeds."

Stiffed: No tip or an extremely small tip.

Side work: Necessary work done by restaurant employees before and after dinner service hours (i.e., Steaming spots off glasses, resetting the tables, cleaning the espresso machine, vacuuming, collecting and refilling oil bottles and sugar bowls, etc.)

Skating: When an employee leaves without completing his or her side work duties.

Sommelier: A wine expert employed to assist customers in choosing wine.

Runner: The person who brings out the food to you. He or she also offers fresh-ground pepper or any other condiment to compliment your meal.

Table number: Each table is assigned a number.

Top: Table.

Position number: The location of each diner sitting around the table. Each chair has a position number, usually starting clockwise. As you order, the server writes down your position number so that the runner brings the correct order to that person (e.g., "The position three at the four-top at table two ordered the steak rare.")

Pittsburgh: Meat cooked extremely rare on the inside yet appearing dark and grilled on the outside.

Auction off food: When the runner doesn't know the position numbers for the food and says something like, "Who gets the Bolognese?" Totally unacceptable.

Walk-in customer: A customer without a reservation.

The walk-in: A giant refrigerator in the restaurant with multiple shelves, often in excess of twelve by fourteen feet.

Flip times: A list of seating assignments and pertinent information distributed to each employee before the dinner service begins. This includes, but is not restricted to, the time of the first and second reservation for a table, any dietary requirements for a diner at that table (for example, diabetes, food allergies, vegan or kosher). If it is a special occasion such as a birthday or an anniversary, or if it is the diner's first time at our restaurant, the servers, entire dining room staff and kitchen will be made aware of this info prior to the start of the dinner service.

Turn: One seating completed; food served and customer paid and left. The table is reset and prepared for the next seating. Two or three turns per table, each night, is what's aimed for.

Drop the check: Give the diners at a table their check. This should be done after they've finished their coffee and desert.

Re-silver: Remove soiled silverware and reset with appropriate flatware for the next course.

Crumb the table: Remove all crumbs from the table with a curved, metal crumber.

Wine key: A wine opener/corkscrew.

Server test: A written, verbal and practical test I gave to each server before I allowed them to wait on a table. They had to know all aspects of the menu and be capable of intelligently answering any questions posed by the diner. The practical test involved them waiting on one of my friends, who would be willing to give me an honest critique of their performance.

Line: Where the food is prepared in the kitchen.

No-show: When a customer does not show up for their reservation and doesn't call to cancel.

Nazi list: A list comprised of chronic "no-show" customers and extremely difficult and disruptive diners. These individuals will never be given a weekend or holiday reservation.

Nuke it: Microwave it.

Party: A group of diners.

VIP: A very important diner. It could be a celebrity, a relative of the owner, a friend of the chef or waiter or another restaurateur we want to either impress or treat special.

Spanglish: A combination of English and Spanish we all used to communicate with our non-English speaking employees.

Specials: Each night, there were several specials that were not listed on the menu. The server would either describe the items and prices, or they would be printed as an insert to the menu.

Price-fixed: On certain major holidays, a price-fixed, preset menu is offered, usually presenting a choice of four or five different appetizers, entrées, desserts, etc. This is usually done on Valentine's Day, Christmas Eve and New Year's Eve.

CIA: Culinary Institute of America, a prestigious culinary institute.

Dolce: "Dessert" in Italian.

After reviewing this study guide, kindly turn over your home, cell, parents' and emergency phone numbers, so that we may call you to cover for a missing sever five minutes before the dinner rush. Thank you for applying, and welcome to Sentimento.

Chapter 4

The Many Faces of Christopher Miller, the Schizo Chef

Christopher Miller was our executive chef and possessed more personalities than Sybil.

Christopher was and is a talented chef. We knew him for several years before we hired him to be our executive chef, and during that time I always viewed him as a calm and normal individual. Out of the kitchen, he seemed like an easygoing and likable fellow, although he frequently complained about his incompetent employers and repeatedly stated that "they" did not know how to run a restaurant properly, "they" insisted he use inferior quality of meat, etc. I thought he was probably right and simply venting to sympathetic ears, since I had no reason to doubt his word.

Let me just mention that my husband and I genuinely liked Christopher very much. We spent an enormous amount of time with him and his second wife, Anna. After his divorce from Anna, and before his third marriage, he often came over for coffee or a glass of wine.

He married his third wife three years before we opened Sentimento, yet he always came over alone, unaccompanied by her. Then again, there was the one exception, when she joined us for a drink. He would always explain that the reason for her absence was that she was unable to get a baby-sitter. They had a blended family: his four, her two and their one.

Over the years, the three of us discussed a plethora of different subjects. He appeared to be a pleasant person whose company we enjoyed.

Christopher had worked in many restaurants during those years and would usually contact us when he relocated to a new establishment. We would then regularly frequent wherever he worked, often accompanied by friends. For a very short period of time, he had his own place, which quickly disappeared from the dining scene.

When it was in business, we would dine there at least once or twice a week, often being the only table occupied. We thought perhaps it was a bad location. After a few months, the restaurant was gone and he was MIA from the dining scene. He resurfaced a couple of years later and contacted us.

We always felt that Christopher—God forbid any foolish waiter, busboy or runner called him "Chris" by mistake—just had never been given the right break at the right time. He wasn't a kid, he was a forty-six-year-old man when we opened the restaurant, and he suddenly changed his age to thirty-seven; it should have been the first clue that all of his burners weren't lit.

We only saw his third wife a few times in all the years we were open and then, it was strictly by chance. She enjoyed dropping the kids off at the restaurant during the day, when I was not present, and utilizing the Sentimento waiters and bus staff as though they were day-care center professionals. I mentioned to Christopher on more than one occasion that I preferred she not bring the children unless she planned to stay and watch them. I explained that there were numerous ways for them to injure themselves when they were unsupervised, and after speaking to him about it, the frequency of the drop-offs intensified immediately.

Christopher purposely and repeatedly allowed his brood to run amuck throughout my restaurant, especially in the reception area. They always left the area in shambles, usually knocking over plants and disrupting the décor, coloring in the reservation book and destroying most objects within their reach. It created a terrible situation.

When I arrived at Sentimento, before I could begin returning phone calls, opening mail and checking to make sure that all side work was efficiently completed, I would first have to have someone vacuum the front area again, or on many occasions, do it myself. It would be necessary to reorganize and straighten out the entire waiting area since it appeared as though a small tornado had hit it.

My husband insisted I just ignore the situation because it wasn't worth an altercation. Vincent preferred to win the war, and losing a battle here and there didn't make sense to him. He was wrong!

As time passed, I realized that with Christopher, we were not always dealing with a rational individual. He was arrogant, conceited, insecure, paranoid, ignorant, passive-aggressive, manipulative, schizoid, idiotic and devious. Christopher was a true invalidator and a world-class liar, and one of the most spiteful people I have ever met—however, he was also a talented chef.

When I arrived at Sentimento each afternoon, I usually entered through the miasma of the kitchen, never really knowing which Christopher persona would be greeting me that day. Since I spent much more time at the restaurant than Vincent, he did not witness all the day-to-day drama that I was privy to.

We were very generous in our perk-giving to Christopher. For the first time in his adult life, he had medical insurance for his family. We purchased a cell phone for him, his first, and we paid the bill in order to have the capability to be able to communicate with him during the day, since he refused to answer the phone at the restaurant.

When we found we were still unable to reach him on the cell phone, we discovered he had given the phone to his wife. When confronted, he growled, "She needs it more than I do." Vincent immediately informed him of why we felt that was unacceptable. After a few days of sulking around the kitchen, much like a petulant child, Christopher finally got over it.

We even gave him a major credit card in case he needed to order something for the restaurant and I was unavailable. He did use it for a restaurant, just not our restaurant. He used the card to wine and dine his wife and friends when we were closed, or when he did not feel like showing up at work.

When I questioned him about the expenditures, he claimed they were "restaurant research." I wanted to yank the card immediately when the first bill arrived but

Vincent insisted I let it go and not make a big deal about it. Each month, I carefully scrutinized Christopher's credit card charges. It annoyed me that he had dined at David Burke and Donatella's on three separate occasions. That restaurant, located in New York City and, might I add, within walking distance of Bergdorf's, is one of my favorite dining destinations and Christopher was well aware of it. I openly admit to resenting having to pay for Chef Christopher Miller and his friends' dinners, rather than my own dining there.

What really got my attention was when he had the unmitigated gall to use the Sentimento credit card to pay for his wife's highlights—that's a hair coloring and lightening process for all you masculine readers. I did not say a word to him regarding the unacceptable charge. I simply deducted the cost of her hair treatment from his salary, enclosing a copy of the credit card statement and a signed warning concerning inappropriate use of the Sentimento corporate credit card. Case closed.

In retrospect, I realize now that we made some grave errors where he was concerned. I should have stood my ground with my husband and followed my gut instinct when it came to Christopher, but instead I let Vince call most of the shots. I should have reminded Christopher on a daily basis that it was my hard-earned money that created Sentimento, and the reality was that, like it or not, I was his boss. Unfortunately, I was not accustomed to dealing with a human being as illogical and fallacious as the deranged chef. Over time, I eventually acquired the knowledge and expertise to effectively deal with the majority of his bizarre moods and tirades.

Christopher bitched and moaned about everything. One minute he could be cursing and threatening me in a frenzied and crazed manner, and five minutes later, he would hug me and say, "I really didn't mean anything. We cool?" This scenario played time and time again over the years he was with us. He always insisted he didn't mean any of the horrid names he had called me, always emphasizing how much he really loved me. Occasionally, he realized he had absolutely crossed the line of acceptability and would panic; the fear of losing his job would then create a temporary period of "good behavior."

When Christopher occasionally felt extraordinarily courageous, he would take a crack at verbally challenging Vincent in front of the other employees. Vincent would quickly put the diminutive chef in his place. A typical verbal confrontation would usually be initiated by Christopher as he mumbled an obscenity, directed at Vincent, just loud enough to be clearly heard.

One of the first times it occurred, I was actually shocked at the manner in which Vince responded. I was sitting at the computer in the tiny, makeshift basement office when I overheard Christopher talking to himself—

or, at least, I thought he was talking to himself. I was unaware of the fact that Vincent was also in the bowels of Sentimento.

Christopher clearly stated: "I'm working my fuckin' ass off to make you two motherfuckers more fuckin' money. You'll see, asshole, I'll fix you! You're gonna be one big, sorry fuck when I'm done with your guido ass!"

My husband is extremely intelligent and always in control. I have no idea how he maintains this control but he rarely ever allows his emotions to rule him. However, on this particular occasion, he reacted extremely out of character. I was shocked when I suddenly heard Vincent yelling.

"What did you say about me? Do you have something you want to say to me?" He shouted this as he ran up the basement stairs after Christopher.

Vincent continued to yell: "If you have something to say to me, turn around and say it to my face like a man!"

Christopher froze in his tracks on the steps, hesitated a moment, and stammered, "What are you talking about?"

"What am I talking about? You must be joking! Who do you think you're dealing with? I am not one of your little lackeys! I am YOUR EMPLOYER! Do you think I am afraid of you? Do you think you are capable of intimidating me in any way, shape or form? If you do, pal, you are sadly mistaken, and get ready for a rude awakening!"

By now, I was out of the office and halfway up the stairs and was standing behind Vince. My husband continued following him up the stairs as Christopher bolted toward the door leading to the security blanket of the kitchen. Christopher obviously was hoping the kitchen would offer some form of sanctuary. He incorrectly assumed that Vincent, being the refined, educated and classy guy he was, would never bring this altercation into the kitchen and in front of the assembled kitchen employees.

"Don't you ever speak to me like that again!" Vincent yelled. "Turn around and look me in the face! Be a man! Don't you have any manners or common sense? Did you actually think I would ignore this? You are rude and childish! If you're going to act like an immature and spiteful child, that's fine with me, but you're going to be treated like a child who can't control himself—and believe me, you will NOT work here any longer! Is that what you want? Because that's what's going to happen if you keep this up. You are losing the respect of the entire staff. If you really think we're so terrible to you, why don't you just leave? You know where the door is. We'll survive and I'll have another chef here in an hour!"

He said this with great emphasis on the word "another," snapping his fingers sharply as he stated it.

Christopher stood there dumbfounded. He had not anticipated this. He never expected to be confronted by Vincent, let alone humiliated in front of the entire kitchen staff and after about thirty seconds, he innocently asked, "What do you mean?"

"You know exactly what I mean," my husband responded. "I am tired of listening to you pontificate on your grandiose culinary attributes! Either get with the program and apologize or move on! I'm done putting up with your bullshit and I don't make idle threats!" Vincent paused a moment while the kitchen staff stood mesmerized.

Then he went on: "You better take a minute to think about your options and make a decision, buddy. Remember to consider the possible ramifications of whatever you do next."

That being said, Vincent left the kitchen and went back downstairs to the office. By this time, I was in the kitchen, along with every stunned employee. Christopher stood dazed and confused, and then seemed to realize he was in deep doodoo and had better do some immediate damage control. He headed down the stairs.

I closed the door leading from the kitchen to the basement.

"The show is over. Let's get back to work. It's four o'clock and we'd better be ready to go at five," I said.

I walked out of the kitchen and headed for the dining room. I was an internal wreck and utilized all my self-control to keep my hands from shaking. I didn't know what was going to transpire between Christopher and

Vincent and had no clear conception of what would be the ultimate resolution of the confrontation. I proceeded to the front of the dining room to prepare for the dinner rush. I prayed I would have a chef when it began.

Meanwhile, Christopher remained downstairs in Vincent's office for what seemed to be forever. Eventually, Christopher resurfaced and resumed his station at the head of the line.

Basically, Vinnie had told Christopher to "shit or get off the pot." He informed Christopher that his behavior was not only unacceptable but that it was affecting the efficiency of the restaurant and causing a morale problem with the other employees. Christopher vowed to improve his attitude and behavior. He said, "It's not my fault! I'm under a lot of fuckin' pressure. I didn't think you'd get so fuckin' upset."

Crisis averted! This was one of many of Christopher's verbal challenges. On this particular occasion, Vinnie went out of his way to continue the altercation in front of the staff in order to make a point, not only to Christopher but to the other employees as well. The message he was trying to relay was, We will not tolerate this type of inappropriate behavior.

Although Christopher may have been in many ways a genius in his artistic domain—the kitchen—he was an imbecile in just about every other aspect of his life. He was mean-spirited, hypocritical and behaved in an utterly misogynistic manner. From what little information he provided, he did not have a positive relationship with his family. Unfortunately, it appeared as though whatever childhood baggage he was still dragging around, I was the official Sentimento recipient of the hostility he felt toward women.

The atmosphere I attempted to create at Sentimento was one of mutual respect and good will, but when it came to Christopher, I failed miserably. To the best of my ability, I endeavored to do whatever was necessary to make the best of a bizarre situation.

Before we opened, as I previously stated, Christopher and I were very close. While the subcontractors were busy working to finish Sentimento, Christopher and I spent all day together, week after week and month after month. I was there to make sure details were correctly implemented and he was there because, against our advice, he quit his job two months ahead of the schedule we had planned. I listened with a sympathetic ear to all his problems; I tolerated the way he blasted show tunes and Tori Amos on his ancient boom box, and I acted supportive at all times. Since we were stuck paying him anyway, we had him remain at the site so I could come and go with a modicum of confidence, hoping that he could accept deliveries and keep an eye on things.

Once, when I had stepped out for an hour he refused to accept an important package. When I inquired as to why he refused the delivery, he merely looked at me with a blank expression, much like that of a deer caught in the headlights of an oncoming car, and shrugged. This occurred shortly before we opened the restaurant, and I rarely left after that.

I hired an experienced kitchen designer to consult with us on the planning of the kitchen in order to create optimum efficiency and flow. We had him meet with Christopher on numerous occasions and gave our chef the option of requesting any item for the kitchen he deemed important. I purchased every special piece of equipment and cooking utensil he requested. I installed a giant exhaust system and air conditioning. I made sure I provided everything he requested as long as it was within reason; however, I felt the plasma TV and cable (with HBO) he requested were not within reason. I allowed his input into the shape of the plates and anything else he felt strongly about. In other words, I was a schmuck with deep pockets.

We had what I thought was a nice friendship and a relationship that both my husband and I valued. We wanted Christopher to be involved in some of the decisions and went out of our way to demonstrate that we respected his opinion. Shortly before we opened, he began behaving extremely hostile and abusive to our staff and to me. Initially, I thought he was merely nervous about the impending opening of Sentimento, but what I failed to realize was that he was nuttier than our almond biscotti.

Christopher behaved in a horrid manner to the majority of the staff on a daily basis. His frequent temper outbursts caused me to lose many talented servers and cooks. They could only endure his particular brand of abuse for so long and then they would either approach me for assistance or quit. The few times Vince or I attempted to intervene, the result was disastrous. Christopher would then attack his victim in an extremely vicious verbal assault.

He once screamed at a waiter, "You'll never travel the Hershey highway again when I get done with you." He went on to explain that he was going to rip the waiter's face off and feed it to the dogs. I never did find out what he was referring to, since I was totally unaware that there were any face-eating dogs lurking around the neighborhood.

More than often, he just would physically threaten them. It was a ludicrous statement since he was merely a tiny man with a huge Napoleonic complex. He was only a few inches taller than my petite frame and I am fairly confident that I could have decked the bastard if the situation arose.

Christopher was not discriminative in his torture methods. He would move from one chef to another, verbally assaulting each, and then victimize any random kitchen employee who might be innocently whistling as he went about his work. He was extremely homophobic and went out of his way to harass the gay employees in a most offensive manner.

One of his favorite targets to humiliate was a young chef who was extremely overweight and sensitive about his obesity. Although insecure in his appearance, Barry was arrogant and thought he was superior to all the other employees because of his family's wealth. He was egotistical and obnoxious but still, emotionally fragile.

Barry was always the first to leave at the end of the night, long before he should have. He would strut out through the dining room, while there were still many customers present, carrying his knives in his very own monogrammed carrying case, which was how he earned the nickname "the Ginsu man." He would regularly make fun of the waiters, ridiculing them in any way he could think of, or often refusing to give them their orders in a timely fashion.

Barry kissed up to Christopher to his face and bitched about him behind his back, causing him to be a prime target in the loquacious nature of our kitchen. The chefs would immediately inform Christopher, embellishing whatever Barry had actually said. Christopher could have put a stop to Barry's infantile behavior at any time, since Barry was terrified to actually have a confrontation with our tyrannical executive chef, but he chose not to. Christopher enjoyed the daily drama that would ensue.

I, myself, had experienced my own differences with Barry. I didn't like his attitude and I was getting tired of protecting him from the wait staff, who all threatened to "beat the shit out of him" at least once per night. I eventually convinced Barry to change his behavior or I would have no alternative but to "rethink" his position.

Vincent and I had a meeting with him after hours one night, so that he would not be embarrassed in front of his co-workers. The next day, I could not believe the positive change in him. He was no longer as obnoxious and didn't cause half as much trouble with the servers. It wasn't perfection, but it was a step in the right direction.

Barry's rebirth enraged Christopher, sparking a campaign of brutal humiliation. Barry, a graduate of a prestigious culinary institute, suddenly became the focus of Christopher's entire wrath. He berated him constantly, recruiting the entire back of the house as his military unit against "the Ginsu man." Poor, pathetic Barry began making numerous mistakes and losing outnumbered battles.

When Barry finally cracked, it was on a Saturday night, during the Valentine's Day rush. The drama had actually begun the night before, when Barry had made a serious error in judgment concerning an overcooked steak. Christopher, of course, exploded and the scene escalated into a series of fireworks. Christopher's voice reached decibels I was unaware that a human voice could achieve as Barry's face turned the color of a pomegranate.

Valentine's Day is one of the busiest restaurant days of the year, and it was also a Saturday. In this business, you come to work on a Saturday if you are half dead, have two broken legs and your arm is in a sling. This fact is imprinted into your psyche, both at the culinary institutes and by your co-workers when you secure your first restaurant employment. Everyone works on Saturday. Excuses are unacceptable and if you don't show up, you are fired no matter what your position—from dishwasher to sous chef to head waiter. No one is exempt on a Saturday night.

For a chef to walk in on any Saturday and quit, the situation has to be unbearable. Barry had lasted longer than most on our firing line and had taken more than his share of crap from El Excellenti the dictator. Frankly, I couldn't blame him.

After Barry made his untimely exit, new chefs stayed for two or three months, but would ultimately resign after a few blow-ups with our chef. They would give their notice and that was that.

Eventually, we hired a young chef right out of culinary school, a CIA graduate. His name was Anthony, a husky guy who was extremely timid and very serious. Vincent and I did all we could to make the pensive young chef feel comfortable in the vicious kitchen environment.

We often praised him in an effort to boost his confidence in the hopes that he would relax and stay.

Anthony lasted three months. Christopher tormented him verbally on a regular basis until he would literally cry. It became a bizarre yet frequent occurrence to enter the kitchen and witness one of my cooks openly weeping while Christopher stood there watching with a demented grin of satisfaction on his face. Anthony eventually resigned but behaved like a man and stayed for the entire two weeks' notice, despite the tension and grief he took from Christopher.

Christopher seemed to have the most resentment toward any CIA graduate who entered our kitchen. His own educational background was murky at best and he told different people various fabrications of his own curriculum vitae. There was the tall tale that he had been a successful and famous lawyer who had become disenchanted with the legal system and abandoned the law to become a chef; and, there were the stories of his days at CIA, which he eventually admitted he did not attend. My personal favorite was the fictional saga of his life as a professional martial arts instructor and international champion.

Frequently, I would arrive at work only to be informed that a busboy, runner or server had gotten into an altercation with Christopher, quit on the spot and walked out. They would usually call me to apologize and give me their version of what transpired, explaining that they couldn't endure his abuse any longer. I was often busy writing positive letters of recommendation for these former hardworking employees.

We once had a very good busboy, Willie. He was very dependable and had applied for the position because two of his cousins and an uncle were also employed with us. Willie was a slightly built individual and although he was thirty-three, he looked about twenty. Christopher took an instant dislike to him for no apparent reason and Willie did his utmost to stay out of his way.

One busy Sunday afternoon, when I arrived, I immediately sensed something was extremely wrong. No one was speaking to each other and there was no random Sid Vicious, Patsy Cline or Ramones song blasting through the speakers in the kitchen.

As I approached the dining room, there was an eerie aura of quiet. The runners were quietly folding napkins and there was not a busboy in sight. Usually, during downtime, there was music playing, and loud chatter and laughter as everyone prepared for the dinner rush. The quiet was deafening. On Sundays, my staff was usually busy sharing every sordid detail of their Saturday night after-work adventures.

The fact that Christopher was happily smiling and whistling was the scariest aspect. I knew as soon as I saw him that he had victimized someone.

Through minor Nancy Drew investigation tactics, I had

the full story, in Spanglish, in about ten minutes. It seemed as though Willie had been putting the loaves of bread into the warmer and chatting in Spanish with one of his cousins when Christopher began screaming at him. He had told Willie he was forbidden to speak to anyone in the kitchen, especially to his cousins or uncle. Willie had protested and stood his ground. A verbal barrage of threats and profanity had exploded out of Christopher, and Willie had stormed out.

Later, when Willie saw me up at the podium—he had been across the street, waiting for me to approach my station—he called from his cell phone to apologize and explain. The other employees had already related the identical story, so I knew Willie was telling the truth; even Christopher himself admitted that he had banned Willie from speaking in the kitchen. He then added a few additional demented comments.

Retaining such a toxic and ruthless individual as my executive chef may seem ludicrous, yes, but Christopher Miller was a talented chef. We desperately attempted to improve our relationship over the years, all to no avail. Vince and I had numerous meetings, after-work cocktails and dinners with Christopher. Things would improve temporarily, but the hostility would always resurface in a few days.

I'll never know why he resented us so much or what caused the endless antagonism, especially toward me, but his bitterness was dangerous. We supplied transportation when he totaled his car; gave generous Christmas and birthday gifts and yearly incentive bonuses; and even lent him money on several occasions. Still, he demonstrated animosity toward us.

Eventually, we gave up trying. We learned over time that many talented chefs are high maintenance—not all, but many. Unfortunately, Christopher was an egomaniac who would certainly benefit from daily doses of Zoloft, Prozac or lithium carbonate.

We insisted Christopher interview and hire the kitchen staff himself. We would have the final say if, for some reason, we didn't think an individual was qualified, but since we let Christopher reign supreme in the kitchen, we allowed him to hire the line cooks and other chefs.

Christopher hand-picked his sous, sauté, pasta, pastry and grill chefs. He always ended up fighting with them all night until the "Cold War" began and the inevitable explosion occurred…though of course, it was NEVER really his fault.

Christopher caused me much unwanted grief and aggravation over the years, and during that time, I would often fantasize about adding Prozac to the soda gun located in the kitchen. Perhaps my line cooks and chefs would have been properly medicated and pleasant at all times, had I strategically executed the plan properly.

No matter how bad the insults, threats and histrionics were on a particular evening, most of the kitchen staff ended up drinking together at the end of the night. The dishwashers, runners and bus staff usually drank beer outside the back door of the restaurant in the alley, and the cooks and chefs usually went to a place called Buddy's.

The waiters or servers were an entirely different story. Usually, around eleven o'clock p.m., they would run to the back of the restaurant to use their cell phones and find out which bar everyone was going to that night. They would be completely manic as the shift began to end, feverishly text-messaging each other.

Despite the screaming, cursing and threats coming from Christopher, he would sometimes join them for a drink. Occasionally, even Vince and I would come along and pick up the tab for the group in an effort to promote good will, fellowship and a general sense of camaraderie.

I never really understood how they could fight all night and say "fuck you" every other minute only to party together at the end of each shift. The hostility usually resumed the next day.

I often miss the original chef Christopher Miller I first met in 1990. He was wonderful! He was funny, charming and believe it or not, extremely affable. He was a friend, and I miss that Christopher. I have no idea where that person went or why, but the Christopher I once knew only made rare and unexpected appearances during the five years we worked together at Sentimento.

Chapter 5

The Food Chain—
Executive Chef to
Dishwasher

The restaurant business is a demanding and relentless service-oriented profession and at the top of its food chain, with the exception of the owner, is the executive chef. In my opinion, many chefs are similar to the high-strung diva from *The Phantom of the Opera*, La Carlotta.

Many believe they possess a virtuoso talent, equal to none, and mine was no exception. My chef had regularly scheduled temper tantrums and often displayed the maturity of a three–year-old. When we first opened, he managed to alienate quite a few customers due to his overdeveloped ego and his mulish defiance of preparing food as requested by the customers. After a few unpleasant incidents, we rectified the situation.

Everyone probably thinks they know what busboys do. You might notice when they come to your table and pour your water, sometimes drop off bread and then clear the dirty dishes when you have finished your meal. True, they do all of those things, but much more, too. They are not at the very bottom of the food chain, but close. The dishwasher and the guys who wash the floors at the end of the night are actually at the very bottom.

Let's say your restaurant opens at five o'clock p.m. That generally means that you need your servers, runners and busboys to report to work by three-thirty to start the side work—which is boring and tedious, yet vitally important in the efficient running of the restaurant.

Each table has to be reset if it's not already done, the restaurant vacuumed, the bathrooms cleaned, silverware and glassware checked and cleaned, and both waiter stations must be reset as well. The waiter stations hold coffee pots, glasses, sugar bowls and creamers. At each station, there are point of sale(POS) computers to punch in orders to the kitchen and print customer checks. A small refrigerator is usually built in under the counter to hold milk, bottled water and cheese.

The espresso and cappuccino cups and supplies are also stocked there, along with extra bread plates and silverware. When the staff arrives, this area needs to be restocked; although it is supposed to done before the staff leaves at night, it is rarely restocked and cleaned properly.

This really shouldn't take very long if done efficiently; however, only the busboys and runners actually show up on time to begin. The waiters all act like prima donnas when it comes to side work and will do almost anything to avoid it. They usually would show up anywhere from fifteen minutes to an hour late, with some of the biggest bullshit stories imaginable as excuses.

Almost all my waiters relied on cabs as their primary means of transportation, since most of them had lost their licenses due to DUIs. Many of their excuses were quite creative and imaginative, although, "The taxi was late" was the most frequently used defense to justify their late arrivals.

My busboys and runners were from Costa Rica, Mexico and Guatemala. They rode to work on bicycles and were never late. It could be pouring rain or mid-blizzard and they were on time. These young men were hard working, dependable and respectful.

I was fortunate enough to have hired Miguel. He was very fluent in English, had excellent penmanship and was extremely hard working. He came to work at my restaurant at three-thirty p.m. but started his "day job" at five a.m.

Miguel was married and had a small child. He took on many additional duties that saved me many hours of extra work each week. He took over part of the inventory monitoring, keeping track of broken glass and silverware shortages.

When I came in to work each afternoon, the first thing I would do was check the bathrooms. While Miguel worked for me, they were immaculate. One of the most valuable advantages Miguel brought to my restaurant was having him as my eyes and ears when I was not around. Thanks to his ability to appear invisible, he kept me informed as to which waiter was drinking behind the dumpsters, who was doing drugs in the bathroom and who was sleeping around with whom. No one wants to pick up someone else's slack while their co-workers are having sex behind one of the walk-in refrigerators.

Thanks to Miguel, I knew who was stealing and what nasty little plots Christopher and his merry band of men were cooking up.

My restaurant was a "pooled house" when it came to tipping. All the tips of the night were put together and the servers received the largest percentage. The runners and busboys received the same percentage, plus they all received an additional hourly salary.

Miguel was like a hawk when it came to tips. He could immediately spot tip shortages and identify which server was stealing from the other waiters. I rewarded Miguel monetarily for his snitch services, especially for his willingness to risk a beating from his co-workers for ratting on them. He was a great evaluator of prospective busboy and runner applicants, and would always know who was fluent enough in English to perform dependably in the dining room.

There is an "underground" of busboys, runners and kitchen workers. They have left their countries, families and friends to try to better themselves and earn money in the United States. They all live together in large, rundown houses, ten or twenty per house, depending on its size.

There was one area where the Costa Ricans resided; down the block and over two streets was the Mexican section; and to the left and down another block was the Guatemalan area. These streets were easily identifiable by the ten to fifteen bikes chained and locked up in front of each house.

These industrious young men knew everything that went on in every restaurant in town, since one of their cousins, friends or roommates worked in just about every dining establishment within ten miles. They knew how many dinners every restaurant served each night, what owners were stealing from each other and which establishments were about to go under.

Before a restaurant was about to close down, I would be besieged by busboys and assorted kitchen employees looking for work. In the restaurant business, they were like the rats who are the first to jump off a sinking ship. They weren't going to sit around and wait for the ship to sink or their checks to bounce, and take the chance of not getting paid.

By the time Miguel decided to return to Costa Rica, we employed half a dozen of his relatives, each one personally trained by Miguel. For the four years he worked for me, he was busy saving money and purchased a small taxi company in Costa Rica when he returned home. My husband figures he must be the president of Costa Rica by now.

Over the years, I was very lucky to have wonderful runners. The best runner I have ever employed I hired as a busboy the first month we opened. He was about twenty-four years old when I hired him and he immediately demonstrated such a refined and genteel manner, I immediately promoted him to runner.

A runner is the person who actually brings the food to the table. It is his or her responsibility to make sure that your plate is properly garnished, the food is hot and not auctioned off at the table, and that the right order goes to the correct customer. Each table in a restaurant has a number, as does each chair position. For example, you might hear a chef yelling in the kitchen, "Get me a fucking runner NOW! Table ten's position two's lamb shank is fucking ready NOW!"

Now, let me state that although a runner is dressed the same as a busboy, they are by no means treated the same. The busboys are often treated as the low men on the totem pole, with only the dishwashers beneath them. The runners may deliver the food to the dining room and appear to be working in the dining room, but in truth, they belong to the chef and live a double life. They work half the time in the kitchen and the other half cheerfully and efficiently delivering the food to the customers, checking to see if they require additional cheese, pepper or some other condiment, and wishing them an enjoyable meal.

The chef and the rest of his demonic men working the line treat the runners like gold compared to how they treat the busboys. The runners are considered "one of them." A good runner is one who can anticipate the chef's needs at all times, is able to keep one eye on the board, one on the dupes, and knows what has been "fired" and is almost ready to go out. He is also very often the chef's eyes in the dining room, reporting what's going on at various tables, if there are VIPs or celebrities and their exact locations.

He knows how to multi-task and expedite and how to avoid any chefs who have evil brewing inside them. They do whatever the chef asks, whether it's bringing him coffee or soda, or running around the corner to see how busy the other restaurants are. Although the runner is valued by the chefs, he is ultimately their slave. He lets the chefs know if there are people waiting to be seated, the weather conditions outside and who we are kissing up to.

However, as a perk for that position, the runner is included as one of the guys. He is invited to have a beer with the line after hours and is elevated to their level of testosterone. He is treated as one of their own and not part of the front of the house—which, of course, they all despise.

Chapter 6

The Toxic Employee

The first time I heard the expression "toxic person," I didn't quite get it. However, after having owned a restaurant for five years, I truly learned first-hand the meaning of the phrase; unfortunately, I hired and fired a myriad of them. It wasn't bad enough that I often had no choice but to deal with the toxic customer, but I also had the misfortune of employing them.

When these potentially poisonous people are initially interviewed and employed, they usually seem normal. In fact, often, they appear absolutely fantastic. You may even go around mentally patting yourself on the back for having the insight and intelligence to have snatched them up before one of your competitors grabbed them.

After a week or so, you may start noticing that there is a problem, since truly toxic people can only control themselves so long before their unique form of venom starts oozing out.

Your initial radar goes off when either everyone suddenly hates them or the far worse scenario: everyone loves them and suddenly hates you. Either way, you're screwed and in for some major acid indigestion.

One type is the "everyone hates the new guy" toxic employee. This is the easier scenario to deal with once you have been in the business for a while. As soon as I would start smelling even a hint of their toxic stench, I would start paying very close attention to the dynamics involved before service, during service and especially after service, when everyone was doing their side work.

At the end of the night is when the real grumbling and true feelings of your other employees will surface. If someone is dodging their responsibility and not doing their share of the dreaded side work, you will begin to witness extreme hostility. I would try to be alert, listen and watch. The next day, I'd arrive much earlier than usual and corner one of my busboys or runners, who would spill everything. I was always very fortunate to have, at all times, at least one faithful busboy or runner.

Toxic employees who claim they are working hard and everyone else is jealous of them "because I am the best server" is almost as much fun as a root canal without the Novocaine. I could usually tolerate it for a couple of days in the hope that things would work themselves out, but most times, it was necessary to terminate their employment immediately.

I never allowed my children to get away with whining. I taught them that it was unacceptable behavior at a very young age. They learned that it would *never* be tolerated, and there I was stuck with a staff of world-class whiners. That particular species of toxic employee whines and complains constantly to all of your so-called content and happy staff. Before you know it, all of your employees will have listened to him or her complaining about pooling tips, side work, the kitchen or the ever-popular complaint: me.

Their complaints include a list of crafted plots and creative ideas. They would preach to all my employees that they could be making more money in "the city"—New York City—and that if everyone refused to do what Vincent or I wanted done, my husband and I would have to succumb to whatever their demands were, or they'd all stage a walk out.

I actually had one such toxic employee when we first opened, who actually had the audacity to call a "servers meeting" in the dining room of MY restaurant to plan a mutiny. Fortunately, one of my "loyals" tipped me off to the impending *coup d'état*. I was lucky that all but one server walked away from the revolt. The other servers recognized trouble immediately and distanced themselves from the toxic individual and the grandiose plans.

I fired both the instigator and the one follower in attempts to set an example. I would not be intimidated by idle or genuine threats, and anyone who thought they could do better elsewhere were welcome to leave. In other words, my philosophy was portrayed as "goodbye and good luck and no hard feelings"; however, often, it felt similar to the beginning of a peptic ulcer.

The most toxic of all my employees was, of course, the acidic and demented Christopher. His psyche was a toxic wasteland and his lies, temper tantrums and daily drama would often impede the efficiency of Sentimento. When I look back on the situation, I probably should have fired him, or at least seriously threatened to terminate his employment. I was willing to put up with his shenanigans, always hoping his attitude and behavior would magically improve, but it never did.

Chapter 7

Kitchen Linguistics

The language commonly used in the kitchen of a restaurant, be it a coffeehouse or a first-rate, five–star, fine-dining establishment, is vile. I personally think that as your ratings go up, the language in the kitchen becomes more graphic and grandiose, as both your chef and his cohorts' egos become more inflated.

The assorted use of inventive obscenities is an integral part of any restaurant's kitchen. I have heard the word "fuck" used as a noun, a verb and an adjective; in fact, they have practically conjugated the word "fuck." Of course, I don't want to omit the always popular crowd pleasers "motherfucker," "cocksucker," "fuckin' faggot," "suck my dick," "eat me" and "bite me."

Some of their statements and threats were extremely homophobic and frequently directed at my gay waiters. The snide remarks became so intense that at one point, I actually threatened to send the entire line for a course in acceptable language in the workplace.

Christopher was the biggest offender and leader of the cursing fraternity. I repeatedly explained to him that many of his statements, threats and daily tirades were simply unacceptable. I begged him not to make racist statements and informed him he could never attack a person's heritage, country of origin or sexual preference, or ridicule their physical attributes or lack thereof. None of my pleadings, warnings or threats meant a thing to him.

Occasionally, I managed to put the fear of litigation into his head by telling him he might be personally liable for his derogatory remarks. The problem was, the fear just never lasted very long.

I could tolerate Christopher calling members of my staff and myself "dipshit," "rat bastard," "*pendejo*," "asshole" and even "pussy" was semi-acceptable—

although calling a male chef a "fat cunt," I felt, had most certainly crossed the line.

Due to the nature of his language, I rarely hired women as servers. The women I did employ were primarily pretty college girls in their early twenties, who surprisingly intimidated Christopher. They worked during the summers as runners, and Christopher never, ever treated them in a harsh manner or spoke to them inappropriately. For some bizarre reason, he sanitized his language around those co-eds and even did a little innocent flirting when they were around.

Christopher realized he would have to deal with me if he crossed the line and he did not like dealing with me on this subject—or any other, for that matter, as I could and would out-scream and out-curse him if necessary. There were times when I felt I definitely turned out Oscar-winning performances in front of him, and the fool never suspected a thing. He never understood that I was raised in a Jewish home by a drama queen who knew how to dish out platters of guilt, seasoned with remorse and with just a pinch of confusion for flavoring. Christopher would attempt to take me on verbally about four times a year, much like one's quarterly estimated tax.

On a Friday, Saturday or holiday, when we would do two and three seatings per night, the language would become even more offensive than usual. And in the summer, on excessively hot days, as the temperature climbed over the one-hundred-degree mark, there was no amount of air conditioning, fans or exhaust systems that could ever lower the temperature cool enough in the kitchen to make it comfortable. It was every man for himself, and the tempers flared. The Fourth of July's fireworks were nothing compared to the show that went on in our kitchen during those steamy nights.

One of the more common languages spoken in the kitchen was Spanglish, which, if you refer back to your Sentimento Restaurant Slang Glossary Guide, is a combination of English and Spanish. If I wanted to communicate with my Latin American busboys, runners or dishwashers, I had to brush up on Spanish, learn Spanglish or figure out how to say limpier los banos— better known as "clean the bathrooms."

Someone gave me a copy of a small book entitled *Kitchen Spanish* by Michael A. Friend and T.J. Loughran, and it was my salvation. Although I had taken Spanish in high school, I'd never actually used it, so the book was a giant communication aid. After a while, you start to hear Spanish so much, you eventually begin to pick up a little more understanding of the language.

It really helped me when I hired an Ecuadorian live-in maid to help care for my in-laws, who lived with us. Carmelita didn't speak much English and my mother-in-law did not want to learn Spanish—or any form of Spanglish, for that matter.

One night, a new busboy, Geraldo, kept mumbling something under his breath every time I tried to ask him to do something. The next morning, I mentioned it to Carmelita, our maid. I repeated the word, as best as I could recall its pronunciation. She told me to fire him immediately. To this day, I am not exactly sure of the word's meaning, although I have a pretty good idea. She tried to explain to me that it was worse than being called a bitch—so use your imagination.

That afternoon, as I arrived at work, Geraldo once again mumbled the same thing as he walked past me. The next thing I knew, one of the other busboys, Enrique, appeared out of nowhere, grabbed Geraldo the busboy and dragged him outside, yelling at him in Spanish. A few minutes later, Enrique came back in the restaurant with Geraldo in tow. He apologized to me as Enrique stood there glaring at him.

Geraldo's demeanor appeared to demonstrate sincere remorse for the inappropriate language and disrespect. He also seemed scared to death of Enrique. I accepted his apology; I didn't care if he was apologizing because he was truly penitent or just frightened of the consequences that he would have to suffer at the hands of Enrique. At that point, it no longer mattered to me. I didn't fire him, but instead gave him another chance, and I am happy to say that Geraldo was still employed by me when I sold Sentimento.

One of the more bizarre facts of a restaurant kitchen is the extreme testosterone level of the chefs I employed. They all bragged about how strong they were; whose ass they had kicked or were about to kick; how many hours they could fuck a night and how many different bitches they had already fucked or were about to fuck. "Fuck" and different tenses of "fuck" peppered every sentence; it was their verbal garnish.

They could go on for hours debating endlessly about whom they could beat the shit out of or which server deserved to have the shit beat out of him the most. The subjects ranged from who was the ultimate, superior fighter to who had what color karate belt. For some reason, there was always an endless debate over who was cooler and tougher—Bruce Lee or Jackie Chan. I would be in and out of the kitchen at least twenty times a night and that was always one of the standard conversations going on while the Ramones blasted in the background.

Almost all of my restaurant employees smoked, with the exception of Christopher. The restaurant was a non-smoking establishment and the employees were not allowed to smoke anywhere in the restaurant. I made this rule when a tall line cook set off the fire alarm by smoking a cigarette in the basement. The fire department came charging into the restaurant on a busy Sunday night, demanding that the building be evacuated immediately.

They would not listen to the explanation of what caused the problem while my customers froze outside.

Since my employees—including me—were not permitted to smoke inside, they would walk through the kitchen and out the back door to smoke by the recycling bins. I did everything possible to keep it safe and to prevent the possibility of a smoldering cigarette causing a fire. I filled giant-sized, empty tomato cans with water for cigarette butts in several locations behind the building. When I arrived one day and discovered a can filled with butts and no water, I put out larger cans and filled them with sand, and emptied them myself as I arrived each night.

No amount of yelling or threatening meant a thing to these smokers. They felt that I was just being an alarmist and ignored my pleas; meanwhile, my Nazi landlords were constantly calling me, complaining about littered butts. I was now being blamed not only for the butts of my employees, but also for the discarded cigarette butts that originated from the employees at the business next door to us. It became necessary that both at the end of the night and at the beginning of the shift, one of the busboys and I would go outside, regardless of the weather, and collect the forty or fifty cigarette butts and beer bottle caps, left there courtesy of my staff.

Christopher did back me up on this, since the smell of smoke wafting into *his kitchen* drove him insane. His threats and screams were actually effective with the smokers for at least a week after each incident.

My kitchen line—my pasta, sous and grill chefs and of course, Christopher—were all American. They all had attended prestigious culinary institutes, with the exception of Christopher. He was a genuine, naturally talented chef and I believe he could creatively outdo any graduate of CIA, Cordon Bleu or any other prestigious culinary institute.

Unfortunately, he was his own worst enemy, often alienating those around him. He may have behaved psychotically and or like he was schizophrenic at times, but that in no way diminished his gifts in the kitchen. Although the line chefs changed many times in five years, Christopher made sure they were always replaced by another culinary-educated American.

The appetizer and dessert stations, however, were almost always manned by a diligent person from Costa Rica. I have always felt that in many ways, the appetizer and dessert stations were the most difficult to handle. The men who worked that station were proficient at multi-tasking and handling pressure.

Let's say you have twenty-two tables inside. It's a busy Saturday night in the summer, which means you also have an additional six to eight tables outside and six waiters punching in their orders constantly. At the beginning of the dinner rush, it isn't that bad for the station, because whoever is back there only has to deal with hot and cold appetizers.

However, as the evening progresses, he is dealing with both the appetizers and desserts. The desserts have to be ready for the runners to bring them out at approximately the same time as the servers are bringing the customers their coffee, espresso, cappuccino or tea, while they also have to turn out numerous appetizers, both hot and cold, simultaneously.

Somewhere around ninety people were dining at all times, from around six p.m. to eleven. When the pressure of the appetizers would be over, he would then have desserts to deal with. If you "flip" the tables two or three times during the course of a Saturday evening, you're talking about a hundred and eighty to two hundred appetizers and desserts.

On Fridays, Saturdays and holidays, we would add an extra appetizer and dessert guy—usually a culinary student or a relative of the "salad guy"—plus I would do what I could to help out when it was possible for me to leave my door whore post. That being the case, I would either leave my husband, a waiter or my daughter, if she was around, to hold down the fort while I worked in the kitchen.

The grill, sous and pasta chefs, along with Christopher, worked at a frantic pace during the dinner rush, turning out perfect dishes over and over again. It isn't an easy thing to be able to reproduce not only picture perfect but more importantly, delicious dinners.

My kitchen staff, psychotic as they all were, was always capable of producing impeccable dinners. It didn't matter if they were hung over from the night before, mad at each other or ready to faint from the heat; they always worked as a well-oiled machine. Amidst the threatening, Spanglish and occasionally storming out of the kitchen for a fast drag on a cigarette, they turned out a superior product night after night and year after year.

The faces on the line may have changed periodically but the quality of the food and its impressive presentation never suffered. Christopher checked each and every plate that exited the kitchen into our dining room and eliminated any kitchen employee who could not deliver.

I once read an article in a newspaper in which two chefs criticized the show The Restaurant. They stated something to the effect of that it portrayed the restaurant in a negative way and did not demonstrate the "fun part."

I have to agree that *The Restaurant* did not at all portray a realistic view of what really goes on in any restaurant. I only watched it a few times and thought it was extremely unrealistic and staged. Waiters crying crocodile tears so they would get additional camera time was a little much for my taste, as were the various employees' egos, tantrums and immature tactics—although in that department, no one on TV came close to Christopher's histrionics.

First of all, any true reality show about a restaurant would have to be on cable, since the language of the kitchen and the conjugation of the word "fuck" would never pass censorship on network television. Owning a restaurant involves hard work, long hours, sore feet, sleep deprivation and yes, sometimes even fun.

In order to survive in this business, you have to love it, and I mean really LOVE IT. How else could you justify giving up any hope of a social life or spending time with friends and loved ones? You have no possibility of enjoying a holiday and you are forced to deal with the daily bullshit a restaurant owner must cope with, not to mention the enormous monetary investment required to create a new and exciting dining establishment. You must know how to deal effectively with foul-mouthed liars, thieves, alcoholics and drug addicts…and those are just your employees.

My kitchen staff was volatile, much like nitroglycerin: If handled improperly and carelessly, there could be a huge explosion. I did my best to handle them gently and delicately in an effort to avoid any detonation.

Chapter 8

The Family Meal and Miscellaneous Bullshit

Most restaurants have what is referred to as the "family meal" for their employees. At Sentimento, at the end of a dinner shift, one of the cooks prepared the family meal for the servers, busboys, runners and dishwashers. It was usually a pasta dish such as *quattro fromaggi or rigatoni norma* during the week, but on Sunday nights, it was always something special—such as steak, crab, lobster or shrimp.

Since we were closed on Mondays, unless we had a wine tasting dinner or a private party, we would use whatever was left over from Saturday and Sunday night for our family meal. We did not hold fish or fowl over until Tuesday; we served it to our staff while it was still fresh.

The chefs always ate before the dinner rush and never took part in the family meal. Christopher would always have something special for them around four p.m., to remind the rest of the staff who was important and who wasn't. I know he purposely did it that way because he was quite explicit when he informed me of the true reason.

Christopher would leave each night after the last entrée order came in. He never said "good night." About once or twice a month, when I would come in to work on a Sunday, I would not see Christopher and that meant he had decided he just was not coming in to work. It was his way of attempting to humiliate me in front of my employees; his way of punishing me.

He always refused to inform me in an effort to demonstrate his importance; after all, I was only his boss and the restaurant owner. On these occasions, every employee from the dishwasher to the sous chef had been informed in advance that he was not coming in.

The first time it happened, I actually asked where he was and the smart-ass sous chef informed me that Christopher was taking the night off and that he was in charge of the kitchen. When I informed Christopher that it was unprofessional behavior and that I should have been informed in advance, he said, "Tough shit. Bite me."

I never again mentioned to him his little Sunday high jinks of being a no show. Every few Sundays, he was a no show. From then on, I used my underground pipeline of informants to keep me up to snuff, so that I would know exactly when he was going to pull one of his power plays by not showing up.

After a while, I began to look forward to the Sundays he pulled a Claude Rains. The kitchen staff was far more relaxed and friendly; the waiters, busboys and runners were actually cheerful. I played with the idea of giving him every Sunday off, thus reducing my overhead by lowering his salary, but my husband was adamantly opposed to my suggesting it. He knew that Christopher would never go for making one cent less.

I proposed it anyway, pointing out to Christopher that this would give him the opportunity to spend more quality time with his family, which he constantly bitched to me about. "I'm working my fucking ass off!" He would repeatedly snarl this at me and it became his constant mantra.

I thought having Sundays off would give him a viable alternative. After suggesting this, he stopped taking off Sundays or any other day without informing me first. It seems it was only worthwhile if it pissed us off, and my suggestion and supportive demeanor caused him anxiety, and he panicked. Although this marked the end of tranquil Sundays, I had succeeded in making my point.

I am a stickler for details. Little things like freshly ground pepper and sea salt at each table were important to me. Each napkin being perfectly folded into a fan at each place setting, silverware perfectly lined up and the crystal wineglasses sparkling were just a few of my control issues.

I tried to make my restaurant the type of establishment that thought of everything. If you forgot your reading glasses, not to worry, I had a large container of reading glasses of all different strengths and styles appropriate for both men and women. If you forgot your cell phone and needed to make a call, I would bring a portable phone to your table. Birthdays and anniversaries were treated accordingly, with candles and singing by our staff. Anyone wishing to have flowers delivered to that special someone as they were dining was efficiently dealt with.

Among my personal touches, I was obsessive compulsive about the cleanliness of the restaurant—

especially the bathrooms, of which there were three: a men's room, a unisex disabled facility and the over-the-top beautiful ladies' room. Each rest room had beautiful tile floors and lovely wallpaper but the ladies' room was sensational! I'd even had clouds airbrushed on the ceiling, along with a twenty-four-inch border of cherubs.

The room also had gilded faucets, a golden toilet-paper holder and a glass-and-gold shelf for hand towels. I actually installed a beautiful, cherub-adorned shelf for purses. The ladies' room also had a fabulous, large, gold mirror over the sink with matching gold sconces on either side.

I routinely cleaned these rooms myself, not just during service to keep them neat and clean, but each night after we closed; I would personally scrub every square inch of all three rest rooms so that they would sparkle for our customers. Each night before I left, I placed signs on their doors in English and Spanish, informing my staff to restrict their use to the designated staff bathroom. On my way into my office in the basement, I would check on the bathrooms. On several occasions, as I was checking the men's room, I heard Christopher inquiring, "Is the cunt in yet?"

On one particular occasion, when I distinctly heard this come out of his vile mouth, I stopped what I was doing and charged into the kitchen, and with a gigantic smile on my face, I said, "You rang?"

He turned an interesting shade of reddish-pink, similar to the color of a cooked beet. He could not speak; he could not even sputter out a stutter. It was great! Once again, I succeeded in making my point by confronting him and catching him off guard; in doing this, I avoided an altercation.

Invariably, the bathrooms had to be cleaned again before service, since by the time I arrived, the miscreants I employed had disregarded the signs and done everything but shower in them. There would be toothpaste and hair mousse smeared all over the sinks and mirrors, along with shaving cream and soapy water splashed all over the sinks and floors.

I often wondered if my staff actually had bathrooms in their homes. The employee dressing room was always covered in piles of discarded clothes belonging to my employees. After a while, the room would start to smell a bit gamey and I would demand that they go through everything and take their stuff home, or I would throw it in the garbage.

I had previously informed my employees of my intentions and given them two days to retrieve their clothing. I'd told everyone that anything remaining was being placed in a trash bag and they would have to go through it themselves and claim their belongings. The pile of clothing was so unwieldy, the door could not be easily opened.

While I was going through the pile with Ernesto, one of the busboys, I made an interesting discovery. I came across three interesting outfits—outfits that could not be attributed to my staff. I held the clothes up and visually examined them as Ernesto, my trusty helper, tried to stifle his laughs. I had actually come across Christopher's kid's dirty karate outfits. Obviously, his wife had confused Sentimento with the laundry. I enjoyed handing them to Christopher and did not wait for an explanation.

Chapter 9

The Dynamic Duo

One of the many things that shocked me about owning a restaurant was that once the free "dress rehearsal" dinner and grand opening cocktail party were over, most of the good friends that we formerly socialized with for many years were rarely seen in the restaurant. They would show their faces three or four times a year, and that was it.

If any of you are considering opening a restaurant, heed this advice: do not count on your friends for business. Unless you are giving out free food, you will rarely, if ever, see your former dining companions in the role of customer. I had many friends who I know regularly dined out two to three times per week, yet would only frequent my restaurant a few times a year.

I don't know why that occurred, since my restaurant received rave reviews from multiple magazines and newspapers in the area, including a rating of excellent from *The New York Times.* In spite of this fact, we rarely saw them as customers; upon speaking with other restaurateurs over the years, it appears to be a phenomenon associated with most restaurants.

Tess and Roger were one of the exceptions. They have been our friends for about fifteen years. Tess is a stunningly beautiful, petite blonde who has been blessed with perfect features and flawless skin, and although she has four children, she has somehow managed to retain her twenty-two-inch waist. When she enters a room, she radiates chic confidence, is impeccably dressed and accessorized to perfection. She is clueless concerning her beauty and keeps her accomplishments to herself.

Tess owns a very successful travel agency and we often travel with her. She always plans trips to fabulous destinations with incredible accommodations. We have accompanied Tess and Roger to many countries, both before and after Sentimento, including Morocco and Italy, and to fantastic events such as the Cannes Film Festival, the Kentucky Derby and the finale of the third season of *Project Runway.*

Tess books vacations for many celebrities and her reputation for creating imaginative and discreet escapes is quite renowned. She is able to waltz into any celebrity venue, be it Bungalow 8 in New York City or The Shore in Southampton, New York. If you are with Tess, you are always granted admission and treated like royalty.

Although Tess radiates an aura of calm, cool sophistication, she on occasion is also devilishly funny and one of the most down to earth individuals I have ever met. Tess and I have had our share of "Tess and Ivy adventures" over the years, including experiencing an episode of uncontrollable giggles on a dock overlooking the Marina Royale outside a restaurant in Marigot, St. Martin. To this day, we can't recall what set us off; all I know is that we started laughing about something and it graduated to giggling, at which point I would equate it to a containable brush fire. Then, it suddenly accelerated into a raging, five-alarm event!

We could not speak; we could not stop laughing and in a minute or two, couldn't stand up straight due to our uncontrollable laughing fit. We ended up sitting on a curb near the parking lot—or, as Roger describes it, "rolling in the gutter" as our husbands kept asking, "What's so funny?"

Tess and I have a close, familial type of relationship and view each other as family. We have spent many holidays together, shared numerous vacations and have been there for each other over the years. When my mother was ill, Tess would drive all the way to the hospital with me so I wouldn't be alone for the midnight visit when she was in ICU. She accompanied me on these late-night visits every night for three weeks, insisting she join me. The truth was, I was glad she did.

When my mother passed away, Tess came to the funeral home to help me make the arrangements. Before we left for the funeral parlor that day, we decided to spread all of my mother's jewelry on the kitchen counter, to choose the proper accessories. That day was one of the most profoundly devastating times of my life and Tess managed to make me stop crying and laugh.

We checked out all the costume and genuine jewelry and Tess started putting ensembles together. My mother loved excess and eccentricity when it came to her accessories, and Tess put together some of the tackiest, over-accessorized looks you can imagine. She said, "Wouldn't your Mom just love if we put all this on her?"

I looked at her and realized that she was serious. She had put together several groups of necklaces, bracelets and rings. In between my sobs I said, "Tess, are you kidding?"

She looked directly at me and said, "I am not kidding! Lilli would love that we are sitting here trying to choose the jewelry she will wear for her final appearance!"

My friend Debi, who was also with us, agreed that Tess was absolutely correct. Debi had actually been with me at my mother's bedside at the end. My mother had adored both Debi and Tess, and I realized that they were right. She would have loved that we were all together, making a corporate decision on her final outfit.

All of a sudden, Tess ran to my bedroom and when she came out carrying the highest high heels I owned, she actually appeared triumphant.

"Ivy, you and your mother wore the same size shoe and you know how she was so sad she couldn't wear heels anymore. She will love these!"

That was when I stopped crying and began laughing. She appeared so earnest and serious. The image of Tess standing there with that determined expression, holding those shoes, will be etched in my memory forever.

She was also an integral part of my daughter Jessica's wedding festivities. She accompanied Jessica and I to help choose the perfect wedding gown, since she had two married daughters of her own. Tess has impeccable taste and panache, and my daughter adores her.

She also assisted with the plans for Jessica's bridal shower. I rented a magnificent mansion that was surrounded by multi-tiered levels of beautiful gardens, surrounded by koi ponds and a huge tranquility pool. We utilized the pool house, complete with a beautiful oak and brass-trimmed bar, for a Victorian garden party. I am proud to say that we dazzled all those in attendance, but more importantly, she helped me provide my daughter with a day she would remember and cherish for the rest of her life.

Roger, on the other hand, is a towering, six-foot-plus kind of guy, with dark hair and eyes and a constant tan. Roger is the owner of an extremely successful rental firm specializing in high-profile social events. He is always involved in any major event that is occurring in the New York vicinity that requires rentals; from movie premiers to foreign dignitaries arriving in the USA, you will see his equipment, canopies and red carpets.

Tess' petite, pale beauty and Roger's giant mountain of tan muscles attract quite a bit of attention when they enter a crowded room. Of all our friends, they were among the couples that frequently dined at Sentimento.

They would usually call to see if we were busy, and arrive close to nine o'clock p.m. during the week, and even later on the weekends. They usually dined at Sentimento with us anywhere from two to three times a week and would try to come as late as possible so that they could dine with us, since we wouldn't sit down to have dinner until the last customer was served. When I would see their name on the caller ID, I would get excited because I knew I would be in store for fun.

Tess had a favorite table—number twenty-nine on the banquette—and Roger would give me grief if it was occupied when they arrived. They usually entered the restaurant via the back door and through the kitchen, which annoyed Christopher. I told them to enter that way since by eight or nine o'clock, there would be available parking in the lot behind the restaurant. They would pass by the garbage and recycling, go down two steps and be in the kitchen. It was a lot easier to enter by way of the back lot than parking three or four blocks away from the restaurant.

Roger and Tess had numerous celebrations at Sentimento, ranging from a large anniversary party for his parents to numerous business dinners and birthday celebrations. One year, on my birthday, Roger had a giant banner made by his art department that read, "Ivy is so old…" It had bullet points that followed:

1) Ivy is so old she was a waitress at the Last Supper.
2) Ivy is so old, her Social Security number is 1!
3) Ivy is so old, she missed the Titanic because her Franck Muller was slow.

He actually listed twenty-five "Ivy is so old" statements.

Roger bragged that he had his entire art department employed, working 'round the clock just to torment me.

During the years at Sentimento, Roger's talents evolved from the simple practical jokes to a virtual art form. Of course, I was not exactly an innocent in that department since before, during and after Sentimento, I certainly performed my share of dirty deeds directed at Roger on his birthdays.

I readily admit to posting giant fifties announcing his birthday all over the front of his house when he turned forty-two, and sending a bouquet of balloons with fifties printed on them to his office the same year. I must state that I did not do that until he told people I was fifty when I was thirty-six.

My shining moment of revenge occurred the year after we opened Sentimento. Tess and Roger had recently completed decorating their very beautiful and formal home, and they had commissioned a custom-made cream and lilac area rug, which cost a zillion dollars. Tess had informed me that this was presently his most cherished possession.

They were the also the owners of four adorable and high maintenance pups: Lola, Roger's "little girl"; Sparky, the sweet boy of the group; Truffles, the youngest of the three pups (who was Prozac dependent); and Duke, the patriarch of the ensemble.

Lola, who was Roger's favorite, was somewhat of an escape artist and would often manage to sneak out of the gated kitchen area. I used this fact to my advantage while planning his birthday surprise.

Because the restaurant was closed on Mondays, the Monday of Roger's birthday, I was free to implement my plan. I spent the entire afternoon searching two different malls for the perfect items to create the perfect prank. I must admit, I did receive some rather strange looks from numerous salespeople as I asked if they carried the items I required.

I was about to give up when I decided to try one more store. I observed that the sales clerk had a slightly unique appearance. She was likely in her mid-sixties, with bleached-blonde platinum hair teased high into a lopsided beehive. She was wearing bright purple lipstick, which was smeared all over her mouth. The large, dangly earrings she wore were adorned with multiple male appendages. I will spare you the other details of her age-inappropriate outfit.

I bravely walked up and asked if they carried the items I required. She responded in a severe, graveled, cigarette voice, "Whatever tricks your trigger, honey. Follow me."

I obediently followed her, while she eyeballed me as though I were the strange one—and finally, voila! I found what I was looking for and hurried out of the store, and made my way home feeling elated. I called Tess to inform her of my gift to Roger, and since I required her to be a co-conspirator, along with her children, I needed to provide her with the covert instructions necessary to carry out my mission successfully. Vincent did not think I could pull it off but reluctantly agreed to participate.

While Roger was at our house with Vincent, I snuck over to his home to set the scene. A few minutes later, Roger and Vincent entered the massive center hallway of their home, since Roger wanted to show Vincent the completed "music salon."

When Roger opened the gilded French doors that led to the room, he froze with a look of horror. In the middle of his zillion-dollar carpet was a small mound of feces, followed by an excrement trail; and in the middle of the room was a huge blob of vomit.

We always teased Roger about being obsessively, crazily clean. He was the sort of guy who would go around putting coasters under your glass mid-party— not as anal as Felix Unger, but a close second. Now, he was horrified to think that Lola might possibly have violated his beloved rug.

Tess and Vincent just stood there appearing dumbfounded, but I immediately offered to help and ran for carpet cleaner. Roger gingerly took tissues and began picking up the feces as he gagged. At this point, Tess and Vincent started to lose it; Roger did not notice, since he was preoccupied with staring at the vomit that had defaced the imported carpet. Roger still did not realize that the feces was rubber, and he actually looked ill himself.

While this scene was taking place, two of Tess' and Roger's children joined the spectators, totally aware of my plan. Roger kneeled on the rug, not knowing how to effectively wipe up the vomit. As my husband was on the floor laughing, Tess was squatting and holding herself as tears of laughter rolled down her cheeks, while the kids photographed their father with a digital camera. Roger was clueless.

Finally, as my cohorts hysterically rolled on the marble floor, convulsed in laughter, Roger remained kneeling on the rug in total confusion. I heroically and arrogantly strutted over and picked up the rubber vomit and scooped up the rubber feces as well.

"Gotcha!" I shouted.

Mission accomplished. I finally was able to get him—but, I might add, it was the last time I succeeded at it.

Chapter 10

Randall Thompson Williams III

I met Randall Thompson Williams III when he wandered into the restaurant with a group of friends late one Friday night. We started talking and before I knew it, I had consented to work at a charity benefit and had committed to donating appetizers for approximately five hundred. I am usually not easily manipulated, however, that sweet-talking Randall immediately convinced me that it was imperative for me to participate in the event. To this day, I am grateful that I agreed to be part of the benefit since it is how we began a close and loving relationship.

Although his birth certificate may read Randall Thompson Williams III, somehow, over the years, the Randall portion of his name evolved into Randee, Dee or Three, and occasionally The Third. My personal favorite, and the way I address all his e-mails, is Randee Dandee. He responds to all versions of his name with an impish smile.

It is hard to adequately describe Mr. Randall Thompson Williams III. When I met him, he was thirty-two and gorgeous! He is tall, blond, muscular and boyishly handsome. The man is devilishly funny, clever, extremely intelligent and dresses very "*GQ*." He is the adored and revered only son of a very socially prominent and wealthy family.

Randee is equally comfortable rubbing shoulders with the rich and famous, hob-knobbing with celebrities or having a drink with the waiters at Buddy's. He is a successful stock broker and one of the most charming and affable people I have ever known. I simply adore Randee and he knows it. Over the years, he has become a close friend.

One thing I may have neglected to mention is that he is gay. His partner in life, or long-time companion, or whatever the politically correct term is today, is an equally gorgeous guy, Dr. Michael Stevens. Dr. Mike, as his patients like to refer to him, is probably the busiest and most sought after gynecologist in northern New Jersey. He is the OB/GYN physician to the rich and famous of the Garden State. Dark, handsome and well over six feet tall, women line up in his office daily and are willing to wait hours in his luxuriously appointed waiting room. He is in such demand that they often wait up to three months just to acquire an appointment and the chance to put their feet into his stirrups.

Mike and Randee are very discreet about their private lives and as a result, neither Dr. Mike's patients nor Mr. Randall Williams III's millionaire customers have a clue concerning their sexual preference.

The darling duo appears to the outside world as two macho stud muffins—hence Dr. Mike's crowded waiting room of flirting pregos, eligible, upwardly mobile executives and lonely housewives. I personally cannot fathom the idea of my ever becoming his patient; it would just be too weird to even verbalize. He often teases me by informing me he has a speculum with my name on it. He enjoys chasing me around, pantomiming an exam while trying to tickle me until I respond with something along the lines of, "Fuck off, Mikey."

When friends of mine discover that Dr. Mike is not only a customer but is also a friend, they actually get excited. I understand he has an exceptional bedside manner and I must admit, he is quite the charismatic charmer.

What really amuses me is the fact that everyone, from Randee's zillionaire customers to Mikey's patients, are always trying to fix them both up on blind dates with daughters, friends or sisters.

My darling Randee had worked and managed restaurants while he was in college and graduate school—he earned an MBA at Harvard School of Business. He worked as a waiter, bartender, cook and manager at restaurants in Provincetown during the summers while he was in college, thus he was very well versed in all aspects of the day-to-day running of a fine-dining establishment.

Randee became my salvation when I had to have a night off, since he loved to be the door whore. He was able to run Sentimento efficiently, without any incidents, and was extremely adept at charming the customers and keeping the waiters sober and working. The kitchen staff would not antagonize him since he intimidated them, especially the homophobic Christopher. Since Randall did not appear overtly gay and was so drop-dead gorgeous, the cretins in the kitchen were confused concerning his sexual preference, and actually went out of their way to please him.

Before he began helping me out by filling in as my substitute door whore, he often would stop by for an espresso before service began or bring me a glass of wine and chat at the end of the night. I did not realize during that period of time that some of my Latino employees were gay—until one night, I noticed a dishwasher checking out Randee's very toned *gluteus maximus*. They would practically drool and salivate as Randee walked back to the coffee station to make himself an espresso or wave to the kitchen staff.

When I brought this fact to his attention, he loved it and would ultimately strut his stuff in front of them, his philosophy being, "If you've got it, flaunt it!" It was amusing to watch as Mr. Randall T. Williams III inadvertently tortured their little souls with lustful fantasies.

My staff, not exactly rocket scientists to begin with, were initially very confused by my relationship with Randee. We always hugged and kissed when we saw each other and were affectionate toward each other. At first, they thought we were having an affair. Randee thought it was hysterical and did his utmost to convince my employees that they were correct in their assumption. It was not until much later that they caught on that although stunningly handsome and macho in appearance, he was in truth a hunky homosexual who was off limits.

If it were not for Randall's help, friendship and loyalty during those five years when I owned Sentimento, my life would have been more difficult. When a frumpy, evil, troll-like food critic attacked me personally in print with false allegations, it was Randee who talked me through the pain and humiliation. He called me the second he read the personal attack and convinced me to walk into the restaurant that night with my head held high and a smile plastered across my face. When Christopher would go through one of his "hissy fit" stages, it was often Randall who would go out of his way to make me laugh.

Over the years, I listened to his advice, valued his opinion and took his critiques seriously. I have always found that I learned more from my mistakes than from empty compliments, and Randee was always open and painfully honest, even when it hurt.

Randall once worked for me for an entire weekend when I absolutely had to fly to California. He also filled my post when I was the first woman to be named Humanitarian of the Year by a local medical center and was honored at a formal gala. When I yearned to go to Tess and Roger's annual Christmas bash, he agreed to be the door whore and only made me beg and grovel for a few minutes before he acquiesced. Sometimes, when he observed how exhausted I was, he would order me to take the night off and attempt to send me on my way, always offering to take over.

It was the illustrious Mr. Williams who created the term pertaining to all things I do as "Ivyesque." I guess the definition of Ivyesque might be "borderline to over the top, yet still tasteful."

For example, he thinks my style of clothes and the

fact that I am addicted to all things Louis Vuitton is Ivyesque. I actually named my toy poodle puppy Louie V and he travels in his very own Louis Vuitton dog carrier. Randee has emphatically stated that the numerous parties he has attended at my home, along with its decorations, are totally Ivyesque. Recently, when my daughter was married, he thought it was the most Ivyesque event he'd ever experienced in his life.

One year, I gave him all my "over the top" costume jewelry to adorn his Christmas tree. He decorates it each year with jewelry and nothing else. Recently, he has been begging me for my old gowns; I am not sure why he wants them, but he is very persistent. He also perseveres in mock attempts to steal my baubles, including what he refers to as the "Sentimento Diamond"; of course, he has two chances—slim and none!

Randee is a unique and funny man. He is talented and hard working, civic-minded and resourceful. Mr. Randall Thompson Williams III is a man you just have to love!

Chapter 11

Restraining Orders, Bail Money, Rehab and My Staff

Over the years, I employed many interestingly diverse individuals. Many stayed with me for years. Some started out when they were in high school as busboys and when I sold Sentimento were attending college. In the five years I owned the business, I only employed three or four women as waitresses since every time I hired one, there was some kind of problem. Sometimes they had issues with their schedules and working weekends; sometimes it was a developing romance within the restaurant, in which case they would quit the minute the romance went sour.

One thing I observed about the wait staff was that they lived a sort of half-life, much like vampires. I recall that Bela Lugosi often referred to vampires as "children of the night" in the old *Dracula* movies, and my servers resembled Bela's children in many ways.

First of all, they have their days and nights mixed up. They sleep all day until it's time to wake up and come to work, so that at three or four o'clock p.m., they are just having their morning coffee. They stay up most of the night drinking—booze in lieu of blood, and usually in a group—and then shortly before sunrise, slink off to their respective abodes, where they sleep the day away, although not in coffins...but then again, who knows.

At any one time, I employed multiple servers named Michael, Jason and Jimmy and at all times, several Johns and Marks. In order to keep the work schedule from becoming confusing, the "Sentimento nicknames" were created. Since we had so many employees named John, we had to create the necessary variations: John, Johnnie, Jack, Jackie, JD, JT and Schultzie.

The most intelligent John actually came with his own nickname—JoJo. He was not only an experienced waiter; he was a college graduate with a master's degree in philosophy. He was a handsome young man, always looked sharp and possessed a photographic memory. The only fly in the ointment was his gambling problem. It was odd to see such a young degenerate gambler.

Many customers would request he be their server when they called to make a reservation. I always tried to make sure it happened because he was so popular with my clientele that their disappointment would be very apparent if they thought he wasn't going to wait on them. Some would come in with special jokes to tell him and JoJo always had an inventory of appropriate come-backs—PG, G or X-rated, knowing to respond with the appropriate rating.

He was extremely bright, possessed academic credentials yet wasted his many talents. Although he was a great asset to the restaurant, I took him aside and informed him that I had friends who were brokers and offered to help him obtain a "real job," one that would utilize his college degrees. JoJo was twenty-six when I hired him and each year on his birthday, he would tell me, "This is my last year doing this. Next year, on my birthday, I'll get a real job."

JoJo was still employed at my restaurant as a waiter when I sold Sentimento.

Once, when he was in trouble with his bookies, he told me he was looking for a part-time job to add to his income, so I made a deal with him. If he came in early every day to answer the phone and take messages, I would pay him fifteen dollars an hour. I taught him how to make reservations for weekdays the "Ivy way," and this enabled me to have a couple hours of much-needed time to myself. It was great for a while, since it behooved us both.

Rather than bore you with all the bullshit excuses I had to endure as to why he would show up two hours late or not at all, I'll tell you that we decided to make a compromise: I would teach another waiter to answer the phone, take messages, make reservations for Monday to Thursday and sell gift certificates, and they would then alternate weeks. One week, JoJo would do it and the next week, one of the Michaels.

The Michael I picked was nicknamed Mikey. His dependability was far worse than JoJo's, but I was so desperate for a couple hours away from the phone, I was willing to put up with it.

JoJo would bet on just about anything. I dreaded football season—actually, I dreaded every season, since there was always something to bet on. I always knew when he was losing long before he told me because the bookies knew the restaurant's phone number. I would always cover for him, telling them he was off or away on vacation, in an attempt to protect him.

Periodically, JoJo would show up at work having been severely "worked over." The bookies were always smart enough not to injure him on his face or hands, so he could continue to work and make payments. Eventually, his problem became so large, he had to borrow money. Several times, interesting, unique and frightening-looking individuals would show up, inquiring as to his where-abouts. Sometimes, when he won a few bucks, he would become MIA. He would disappear with his pals to Atlantic City for a couple of days—where, according to him, he was "comped like the movie stars."

I was willing to put up with all this craziness because he was worth it. The customers loved him, he got along with all the other servers and even Christopher didn't mess with him. I know that on some afternoons, when he was supposed to be answering the phone and taking mes-sages, he was sound asleep on the banquette. Each time he screwed up, he always fell on the invisible sword and accepted responsibility for his actions. He knew how much I despised liars and would always tell me some ver-sion of the truth, apologize and ask me not to fire him. I never did fire him, not even when he called from jail to say he would not be in—after all, he did call.

JoJo was actually somewhat of a legend among waiters in our area. It seems that a year before he came to work at Sentimento, he was employed at a local restaurant that was very large and successful. Apparently, the owner freaked out one busy Saturday night and took it out on JoJo. The pony-tailed owner literally tried to kill him by choking him and slamming him against a counter. The cooks were eventually able to pry him off, but JoJo was injured.

He made it home and his parents took him to the hospital, and a police report was filed. The nut-job owner ended up paying JoJo ten thousand dollars to drop the charges and then a month later, fired him. I had heard the story but initially thought it was a "waiter's urban legend"—you know, like the Candyman or the Jersey Devil—until JoJo showed me a copy of the police report.

JoJo might have been a degenerate gambler, but he was the best waiter I have ever seen, bar none. He could take orders on parties of twenty-five, never write anything down and never get an order or position number wrong. He was amazing. I always thought he would be a great commodities trader, since to be a success in that profession, you require a gambler's mentality.

We had several servers who were aspiring actors. Some were just wannabes, but we had a few who were actually genuine actors—meaning they occasionally had acting jobs where they actually earned paychecks. Most of them just hustled around to get jobs as "extras."

We referred to one of our resident actors as "Mark E." He appeared on *The Sopranos*, *Oz* and *Sex and the City* as an extra, along with our other actor/waiters, "Jimmie J," "Joe D," Lucas and Alex.

Sentimento was a perfect restaurant for all the struggling actors I employed because of the location. We were within walking distance of the Summit train station, which made it very convenient for them to get back and forth to New York City for auditions or to make their connections to Silvercup Studios, where they often worked as extras.

Shortly after we opened, we hired Mark E., who was twenty-nine at the time. Over the years, he worked for us on and off until we sold Sentimento. He sometimes made me crazy with his attitude and I once had a verbal altercation with him behind the Sentimento dumpsters over his schedule. He wanted more shifts and became angry when I refused.

Mark E. used to get in my face, complaining about this or that, and I often gave him a hard time because he whined constantly and would occasionally weep. I have no tolerance whatsoever for whiners. The truth was that although he often grated on my nerves with his hissy fits, he could also be very funny and charming, and he used to make me laugh.

Mark E. was openly gay and occasionally asked me if I could fix him up with one of my gay friends. One night, he approached me and said, "Molly Ringwald has nothing over on Vincent."

I looked at him with a puzzled expression since I didn't have a clue what he was talking about. I looked up from the reservation book and asked, "What's that supposed to mean?"

He looked at me and said, "*Pretty in Pink!*" That night, Vin was wearing a pale pink shirt with a pink and navy tie. Mark E. was rolling his eyes at me and pointing at Vincent's backside. As I previously stated, he made me laugh.

Sometimes he would have disagreements with the other guys and get pissy and moody. He used to get excited when Randee and his friends came in for dinner. Randee usually dined with a large crowd, but always on the late side. Due to Mark E.'s frequent moodiness, their code name for him was "NQ," meaning Nasty Queen—however, they never said it to his face.

Mark E. and I often had disagreements, but he was a good and dependable waiter, and I liked him. I went out of my way to make sure Christopher was unaware of that fact, as I knew this would cause him to torment Mark E. more than usual.

Mark E. would charge out of the kitchen and storm up to me, out of breath, insisting that Christopher must be bipolar or schizophrenic. I never agreed with him or gave any indication that there was something wrong with Christopher. I did, however, on many occasions, advise Mark E. that it might be in his best interest to stay out of the kitchen for the rest of the night.

Mikey was one of the first servers employed at Sentimento. I hired him about two weeks before we opened, along with other servers, so that I would have time to train my staff. I wanted them to feel as though they were on a team—the Sentimento Team!

I almost did not hire Mikey, as I did not care for his appearance during the interview. He was disheveled and appeared as though he required a refresher course in hygiene; however, he persistently called, inquiring about the position. I thought anyone who called that much really needed the job and would try hard.

Unfortunately, as time went on, I discovered he had quite the weakness when it came to smoking weed and enjoyed going on the type of drinking binge that took more than twenty-four hours to recover from. He would sometimes show up so spaced out, I would have to send him home.

He always had some half-assed excuse for his behavior. It was "bad fish" from the diner down the street; it was his allergies; or it was whatever lame excuse he could come up with. Of course, he never once admitted he was hung over from the previous night.

For a short time, Mikey and JoJo shared the phone duty, and when JoJo tired of the extra hours, Mikey was adamant that he could handle it and wanted to continue doing it by himself. I went along with it because I knew he needed the money.

I always felt sorry for Mikey and gave him many more chances than he deserved. My first impression of him when he applied for the job was that he was somewhat goofy looking and did not have the best appearance, which is why I almost didn't hire him. He was short, stocky and resembled an oompa loompa from *Willy Wonka*. Some nights, he made numerous mistakes while punching in orders to the kitchen, which was usually the first indication he had been "smoking" before he came to work—and I don't mean the Marlboro reds that all the waiters smoked.

On more than one occasion, he punched in the table number as the amount of people at the table. For example, rather than punch in FOUR at table TWENTY-THREE, he would enter TWENTY-THREE at table FOUR. Whenever this occurred, it created havoc in the kitchen and created chaos in the middle of service until we were able to clear the mistake and re-enter the orders.

Tess could not stand him. Vincent and Christopher both urged me to fire him, but I refused. I just felt so sorry for the portly little fellow. Continuing to employ him did, however, turn out to be one of my bigger mistakes at Sentimento. I did not want to fire him because I felt he would be unable to obtain another position as a server— or as anything else, for that matter. He did not have a good appearance, he was not a great waiter and he obviously had a serious flirtation with both marijuana and alcohol.

Mikey was twenty-five when I hired him and had already worked at many different dining establishments, unable to sustain employment in any one restaurant. He came from a lovely, educated Jewish family. Growing up, he had been given every advantage, and yet somewhere along the line, he strayed from the program. When he was a freshman in college, he had managed to get himself into some major difficulties. I am unaware of exactly what transpired other than the fact that it had something to do with a DUI and a Porsche.

Mikey once had a roommate, appropriately named Slam. Mikey was forced to relocate when Slam wrecked the apartment. Another roommate moved out without notice and immediately went into rehab, leaving poor Mikey to pay the rent. He was frequently evicted, losing his security and leaving him temporarily homeless. There was always a "poor Mikey" story.

Once, he called me at home on a Sunday. He was panic stricken due to a severe case of the flu. We called a friend who was a physician in order to secure an appointment for him the following day and we ended up providing transportation for Mikey to the appointment, since he lacked a license or vehicle. We truly tried to treat our employees as we would want to be treated, but it was a huge mistake.

In the wee hours of a cold February morning, Mikey and some of his lowlife buddies became so inebriated that they literally fell on their faces and passed out drunk in the street. They were taken to the emergency room by a bouncer from Buddy's, who witnessed the incident.

I received a call from Mikey later that day, still drunk from the previous night of debauchery. He left a slurred and incoherent message on my voicemail, requesting that I come and get him. I did not go; I had just about had it by then.

He was unable to return to work for several weeks due to his extensive facial injuries. Several of his teeth were knocked out, he'd fractured his nose, had numerous sutures and a hairline fracture of his skull. He was a swollen, discolored mess and actually had the audacity to be angry with me for not allowing him to return to work until he had replaced his teeth, the facial swelling subsided and he received an okay to return to work from the doctor.

I had many weird and unusual situations occur with my staff over the years. Roger's favorite Mikey incident occurred the second year we were open. It was an extremely busy Friday evening when one of the busboys told me that Mikey needed me right away. I found him hiding behind the restaurant, by the garbage pails. I had asked Vincent to watch the front when I went to see what was going on. It seems a couple came into the restaurant that had a restraining order against Mikey.

Mikey stated he couldn't go within one hundred fifty feet of them and refused to return to the dining room. He also had restraining orders against them. Meanwhile, Roger and Tess had come in while I was out back with poor Mikey, who was shaking and lighting one Marlboro after another.

When he had bolted out of the restaurant, he had left all of his tables unattended. I immediately split up his section among the other servers and went to tell Vincent what was going on. Roger and Tess were sitting on the banquette, watching the little soap opera unfold. Vincent decided he wasn't going to let dueling restraining orders impact the efficiency of Sentimento and diplomatically asked the couple to kindly leave the establishment.

When the woman rudely refused, Vin informed her that he would have no choice but to call the police and allow them to sort out the sordid mess. While this was going on, Roger and Tess were seated side by side on the banquette as though watching a Broadway show or perhaps a dinner theater.

The young lady was not going to leave quietly, nor was her companion, without informing the entire dining room of what a "shit" Mikey was and how she claimed he had physically abused her. Eventually, they were escorted out of the restaurant, all the while spewing out torrents of obscenities directed at Mikey. Roger and Tess gave Mikey a standing ovation when he tried to slink back into the dining room. Just another night at Sentimento.

For five years, I put up with all of Mikey's many flaws and tolerated his shenanigans and pathetic persona. It turned out that during the last six months I owned Sentimento, he was spying on me for Lorenzo, an individual who wanted to buy us.

I had repeatedly refused Lorenzo's offers; I did not want to sell my dream. When I kept refusing, the man spread stories all over town that he was buying Sentimento. My staff got wind of it and chaos ensued. I assured them that I did not intend to sell, but the damage was done.

When I was informed that Mikey was the employee spying on me, I could not believe it. He was well paid for the information he provided and guaranteed a job. I had begun to notice nearly every day when I arrived at the restaurant that his skanky girlfriend was hanging around the podium and looking at the reservation book. Once, it even appeared that she was copying the reservations. I wasn't terribly concerned, since I had the "real" book. I always left the reservations for the next day at Sentimento and took the "big book" home.

On a Saturday morning, Christopher called in a panic and told me that he had discovered that Mikey was a spy for Lorenzo. I confronted Mikey and let him have it. He didn't even bother to deny it but just stared at me in a defiant manner. I wanted to fire him immediately, but Vincent convinced me to wait since it was Saturday and he was not on the schedule again until Tuesday.

That Monday, the only day of the week we were closed, we were busy doing errands when both of our cell phones began to ring like crazy. Lorenzo was making us one last offer—one that was hard to refuse. Of course, there was a catch; we had to have the closing and be gone by the weekend.

Vincent and I had the biggest fight of our marriage that day concerning the possibility of selling Sentimento. He insisted we take the offer and sell, against all of my protests and wishes. I was furious over the speed of the situation and wanted time to think.

I was also raging at the treachery that Mikey had committed. For five years, I'd protected him from Vincent and Christopher, who wanted to fire him; I did this because I'd felt sorry for him and thought he was a loser who needed protection. I even tolerated his numerous arrests for public drunkenness and disturbing the peace—in fact, I actually helped him obtain an attorney for his many legal difficulties. It just never occurred to me that Mikey might be intelligent enough to be a spy. Vince thinks I should send him a "thank you" note, since we probably made an extra hundred thousand dollars due to his spying.

Then, there was one of the Jasons I hired as a runner. He constantly begged to be a waiter. Eventually, I made a deal with him. If he would remove the studs and earrings from his multiple piercings, including the tongue and eyebrow studs, and refrain from wearing puka shells, I would give him a chance. He complied, cleaned up his act and learned the menu.

Jason became a waiter, but was like a lost little puppy. He was always up at the podium, telling me about his love life and furnishing me with far more sordid details than were required.

That summer, I was injured and my daughter Jessica gave up her entire summer break to assist me, since part of my body was encased in plaster. After about five minutes of listening to Jason, she would literally shoo him away. He would put his elbows on my podium and proceed to tell us all of his problems, night after night. He did his share of whining and out-whined Mark E. by a mile. He constantly complained that I gave him the worst sections and the meanest customers who left the smallest tips.

When I brought it to his attention that perhaps it was his fault and had nothing to do with the customers, he immediately started to fight with me. I looked him in the eye and told him, "Do not blame the customers for the poor tips. Accept the responsibility that maybe they were unhappy with the service or your attitude. Part of your problem is that you are extremely pugilistic."

"That's not true!" he responded. "I took out the stud in my tongue."

I explained that that wasn't what "pugilistic" meant and told him to look it up in the dictionary when he went home. Since he said he didn't have a dictionary, he began to ask the other waiters what it meant, but no one knew. It suddenly became a game with my staff, guessing the meaning; Jessica also refused to tell them.

Finally, Jason went downstairs to my office and asked Vincent, who asked him why he wanted to know.

Jason said, "Ivy said that was my problem and won't tell me what it means!"

Vincent replied, "Well, if Ivy won't tell you, I'm not going to tell you either."

Vincent laughed and went back to work. At the end of the night, while everyone was doing side work, Jason begged me to tell him. I finally explained the definition and he was overwhelmed. After that, every night he worked, he requested a new vocabulary word.

Jason was always looking for a "get rich quick" scheme and eventually left his position at Sentimento. He dropped out of junior college five years into his freshman year. He came to the restaurant to inform me so that I could yell at him. He would frequently stop in to give me an update on his troubles.

When we first opened, I hired a busboy named Daniel. He was very bright and a hard worker and I immediately promoted him to runner. After his junior year at college, he returned to Sentimento, and I trained him to be a waiter. He was excellent.

The only real problem with Daniel was that he had a tendency to behave in an obnoxious and arrogant manner to the other employees. They in turn made fun of him and truly disliked him. He was a born politician and his "kissing up" technique, which was off the charts, pissed off the other employees, including Christopher, who despised Daniel and enjoyed tormenting him.

Christopher would encourage the other servers to beat Daniel up and threaten him. Mikey, who was probably eight inches shorter than Daniel was, took great pleasure in torturing him, since he had no fear of any retaliation. When Daniel wasn't looking, with Christopher's blessing, JoJo would routinely add caper juice to his soda or red pepper to the espresso he was drinking. The waiters would purposely bump into him and try to make him get nervous and flustered, since when he became agitated, his face would turn bright red—and I mean really red, not just a little flushed. He would get so red, it appeared as though he'd overdosed on rouge.

Some nights, the waiters would place bets as to who could get Daniel to turn red first. I tried to make them quit doing it, but I had to be tactful. If Christopher sensed I was protecting Daniel, it would be open season on him. So I would threaten my staff, informing them that if Daniel quit due to their pranks, the guilty waiters would have to pick up the vacant shifts. During the summer, no one was interested in too many additional shifts, so they would behave for a few days before it started up again.

We also had a very friendly waiter named Jim. At that particular time, we had several Jims in our employ, so he became "Jim"; another, we nicknamed "Jamie"; and there was also "Jimmy" and "JJ."

Jim was somewhat overweight. He was a cute college kid with an adorable girlfriend, who would often pick him up at the end of the shift. Although Jim was attending the local junior college, his girlfriend had already graduated from NYU, had acquired a master's and was going to school for her doctorate degree. I liked Jim, as did the other waiters and more importantly, the customers.

Christopher hated him. He called Jim names constantly and if Jim went out back for a smoke, Christopher would lock him out so he was unable to get back in. Christopher thought Jim would have to run around the entire block to reach the front entrance, but Jim wasn't stupid. He would just cut through the business next door when this happened.

Christopher called him names like "fat ass," "dickless wonder" and "fuck face." Eventually, Jim came to Vincent and me and explained that even though he loved working for us, he had taken enough abuse from Christopher, and gave us four weeks' notice. I was sorry to see him leave, but I understood, and appreciated the fact that he worked the four weeks even when Christopher constantly threatened him.

The last time I saw Jim, he had lost forty pounds and was managing the "hottest" dining establishment in the area. He was very happy to see us when we walked in and immediately informed us that Christopher had come in one

night and started calling him names in an effort to antagonize him. He let Christopher know that since he no longer
worked at Sentimento, he would have no problem beating
the crap out of him. Christopher had backed off and left.

At the restaurant, I employed what I called the "brother teams." I would hire one brother and as soon as there
was an opening, they would ask if their brother could
apply. Over the years, we had quite a few brother teams
but my favorite were the Gold boys, Michael and Jason.
They were both in college; Jason was a freshman and
Michael was a senior. Jason was the clown of the pair and
Michael was the quintessential serious big brother. They
were both in the six-foot-four or taller range, and I assured
them that they had jobs for life as long as I needed things
on the top shelf of the waiter's station.

Michael and Jason were always punctual, their
appearances impeccable. At the end of their shift, they
would change their clothes if they had plans and then
would request a fashion critique on the ensemble. Jason
loved to play Texas draw poker.

One Christmas Eve, Tess and Roger were having an
enormous family dinner and desperately needed extra
waiters to help serve the forty-plus people they expected for dinner. The boys didn't mind working on
Christmas Eve and were very excited for the chance to
make extra money before they left to go to Barbados
with their family.

On Christmas Eve, we traditionally started serving dinner early, usually around four p.m., which enabled us to close earlier than usual. That night, when we finished, we planned to stop at Tess and Roger's for a fast holiday drink.

When we arrived, around eleven o'clock, most of their guests were leaving; however, one of Roger's brothers was spending the night with his family, as were his parents.

As we entered, the Gold boys were all smiles, as usual. Michael was busy working behind the bar and Jason was even busier, teaching Roger's brother Mickey how to play Texas hold 'em. The next thing I knew, Vincent, Roger, Mickey and the Gold boys were hot and heavy into poker and I eventually broke up the game at five a.m.

One might wonder how anyone could possibly put up with the shenanigans my staff pulled. Part of the answer was that in general, I found that the majority of job applicants seemed to originate from an unstable workforce. Over the years, I had numerous requests for bail money from desperate employees calling from jail. Twice, I received calls from staff members who had been admitted to rehabilitation centers and were calling to inform me that they would be incarcerated for at least thirty days.

I've actually had people come in to apply for a position blatantly drunk, staggering and reeking of alcohol. The first time it happened, I thought the woman might be diabetic and having an insulin reaction and actually asked her if that was the case; she looked at me as though I was nuts. I realized that most times, I was better off dealing with my own staff, such as it was, even with all their outrageous flaws.

Chapter 12

The Gelato Tasting

Our friend Ronald is one of the funniest people on the planet. Over the years, his antics have made me weep tears of unabashed joy and laughter on many occasions.

We have known Ronald and his beautiful wife Lynne for many years. Our sons became friends when they met in second grade, but that is not how we met. We first became acquainted when our son Shane was in the sixth grade and Vincent was coaching one of the baseball all-star teams, during the championship game.

Their first interaction could be deemed somewhat volatile. It seems there was a dispute at first base during the second inning, over whether or not Ronald's son Justin was safe. Justin was on the opposing team. While the verbal dispute was quite innocent, the boy playing first base suddenly started pummeling Justin with his fists. As Vin and another coach attempted to separate the boys, the aggressive first baseman broke loose from the fat fool restraining him and started swinging at Justin.

Vincent didn't realize what was happening at first, since at age twelve, Justin was already taller than Vincent and his back blocked his view. Suddenly, a behemoth of a man jumped off the bleachers and started running onto the field, toward the altercation. The colossal gentleman seemed as though he was ready to pulverize my husband, since it appeared from his vantage point that Vin was restraining Justin so that the other boy could punch him.

At this juncture, I should probably physically describe Ronald. He is six feet, five inches tall and a big, bulky kind of guy, far from a string bean. His perception of the event was such that Justin was in danger. He approached the scene roaring threats, all directed at Vincent(who is, by the way, only about five-nine). He grabbed Vin by the shirt and lifted him right up off the ground, screaming,

"Are you nuts? What the hell is wrong with you, letting that kid throw sucker punches at my son? I'll kick your scrawny ass and see how you like it!"

Vincent went limp as he dangled two feet off the ground, waiting to see the stars that would surely appear following the punch that seemed imminent. Every coach and umpire charged onto the field in an effort to rescue Vincent. They convinced this hulk of a man that there was truly an absence of malice. He eventually released Vincent, dropping him to the ground. The game continued and believe it or not, a friendship began.

Ron always calls me everything but Ivy. When I answer the phone he will say, "Is that you, Eileen?"

At which point I respond, "No, Herman, it's Ivy."

This dialogue continues and, to cut to the chase, I call him Little Dickie, Herman or Malcolm, and he refers to me as Eileen, Irene or any name he sees fit. He never addresses me by my given name.

When we confided in Ron about our plans to open a restaurant, he was very supportive, although he did suggest we seek psychiatric help immediately. Tess and Roger reacted the same way.

Before you open a restaurant, there are innumerable decisions to make; among them, and paramount to Ronald, was who would be supplying the gelato and sorbets. Every couple of days, a different vendor would drop off dozens of samples in an effort to obtain our business. The day an ice-cream representative had an appointment, I called Ronald to join us for the "tasting."

The representative came in with dozens and dozens of samples in Dixie-cup-sized containers. The sorbet flavors were *incredible*: blood orange, green tea, mango, margarita and cosmopolitan sorbet were just a few. The gelato flavors were fantastic and extensive as well. Ronald, whose sweet tooth is legendary among our friends, thought he'd died and gone to ice-cream heaven. As our primary ice-cream connoisseur, his opinion was crucial to our final decision.

Over the course of the afternoon, we all tasted the samples but no one took it as seriously as my friend Ronald did. He tasted each mouthful as though he were a sommelier sipping a 1962 Chateau Margaux, savoring all of its nuances. First, he analyzed the sorbets, giving his opinion on each flavor. I actually took notes. Ronald is a very thorough fellow and a serious gelato/ice cream kind of guy. He took this tasting very seriously. He did not skip a flavor; in fact, he even took the remaining samples home with him and rushed off after giving his unadulterated honest opinion.

Over the course of the afternoon, Ronald probably tasted over a hundred different flavors of sorbet and gelato. The next morning, he called me to describe in minute detail the extent of the "ice cream headache" and GI distress he'd experienced as a result of the tasting.

Thanks to Ronald's expertise in this area, we decided to go with his recommendation. We also utilized his unique talent when it was time to interview for the position of a pastry chef. Our method of interviewing was another tasting and naturally, we also relied on the discriminating palates of Tess and Roger, since they were also experts when it came to culinary confections.

Ronald often enjoys reminiscing about the enormous ice cream headache. He feels it was worth it!

Chapter 13

Goomattas, Golden Showers and a Very Merry Widow

When I owned and operated Sentimento, it was the "in" place to dine and be seen, especially on the weekends. This was extremely evident from April through October, when we were able to designate a small area in front of the restaurant for outside dining.

Our customers were able to sit outside beneath our awning, dine *al fresco* and enjoy the evening. Our restaurant was on the main drag and the sidewalks, in some areas, were up to twenty-five feet wide. If you were dining outside, you were in plain sight of the constant parade of passers-by.

To this day, I will never fully understand why a husband who is obviously fidelity-challenged and cheating on his wife on a Friday night with some little *chiquita* would have the courage to come to Sentimento and chance being discovered. Even more puzzling to me was why these devious husbands also requested outside dining in a location that would put them on display; this I will never understand.

This was the scenario, Friday after Friday for five years. In fact, we had a demographic of cheating husbands. What I found to be more astonishing was that this cross-section of society would bring their *goomattas*—Italian for "mistresses"—on Friday night and return on Saturday with their wives. In many cases, their wives were acquaintances of mine, and this fact boggled my mind. Did these bad boys want to be caught? Or were they arrogant, self-absorbed scum?

My staff was instructed by me never to acknowledge in any way that the husband had dined with us the previous evening, especially if they had waited on the wayward spouse the night before. One two-timing man would usually arrive with a magnum of Dom Perignon along with his "Friday night special." He was an exhibitionist of

Irish descent who always insisted on sending glasses of champagne to the front for Vincent and myself, not to mention to other random customers while they dined. He possessed a thunderous voice and often greeted acquaintances as they passed by.

This man flaunted his young sweetie. On one fateful Saturday night, he had imbibed a drop too much wine and called his wife by his *girlfriend du jour*'s name. He was unable to effectively create damage control and a barrage of verbal explosives ensued. She threw a drink at him and stormed out, and he ran down the street after her, carrying her brand new, white fox jacket—a guilt present he had given her earlier that night. I later found out that they were getting divorced.

Our restaurant was BYOB and the philandering husband had arranged for a case of champagne and a case of white wine be delivered to the restaurant so that his favorite wine would always be available. We never saw him again after that Saturday evening. Vincent attempted to reach him, leaving numerous messages on his cell phone to no avail. He had abandoned a case of 1995 Calera Viognier and a case of Perrier Jouet Fleur de Champagne. After a duration of approximately one year, Vincent and I decided to adopt the homeless vino and gave it a good home—ours!

Many of our customers were single, educated, successful women in their thirties, still searching for Mr.

Right. A popular practice among these women was internet dating. Vincent and I went out of our way to try to ensure that every customer was treated as a welcomed and cherished guest. We always did our utmost to make sure that these rising career women felt comfortable. Due to their comfort level at Sentimento, they would often arrange for their first meetings with their online dates to be in my restaurant.

We had one customer in particular who was more advanced in the online dating scene. When she began coming in three or four times a week with a different man each time, she explained her dating process to me because she was concerned that I might not think well of her being seen with so many different men.

After our conversation, she would have her prospective dates arrive a few minutes before her. I would personally escort them to the table, chat a little and check them out. She would then call me from her cell phone, at which time I would give her my critique.

On a few occasions, I did gently warn her that there was a buffoon awaiting her arrival, and to brace herself. The woman was an attractive thirty-something dentist. She was an intelligent, articulate, charming and successful woman.

One night, an exceptionally handsome man arrived to meet her. I chatted with him for a few minutes and was very impressed; I thought he was the cream of the crop, so far anyway. I made sure they had a perfect table and instructed JoJo to wait on them. They seemed very compatible, were animatedly chatting and appeared to be "clicking." A few days later, she came in, and I inquired if she was meeting the fellow from three nights ago.

"I never want to see that asshole again!" she screamed.

I expressed surprise, since they had seemed to be having such a good time. She related to me what hc had requested of her while she'd sipped her espresso. It seems he fancied himself an alpha-human. In his mind, since he was an "alpha," he explained to her, in order to mark his territory, she should allow him to urinate on her. He felt that this was perfectly normal, since wolves and dogs routinely urinated in order to designate an area as their own and "mark" their territory.

Needless to say, I was shocked for a number of reasons. First, I had never heard of anyone urinating on their sexual partner, let alone a prospective one. Secondly, he seemed so normal.

The next day, I was telling Tess the story and she casually said, "Oh, you mean he wanted to give her a golden shower?"

I said, "No, he wanted to urinate on her. What's a golden shower?"

She laughed and went on to explain to me that a golden shower is someone urinating on you. I had never heard of that form of sexual gratification. Tess explained that a friend of hers was put into that position a number of years before. I justified my ignorance due to the fact that I was only twenty-one when I'd married and therefore had missed any "golden shower" opportunities.

The following Sunday evening, a *Sex and the City* episode aired about a politician Carrie was dating who, coincidentally, happened to be into "golden showers."

A few months before we opened Sentimento, an acquaintance of mine suddenly became a widow when her husband suffered a fatal heart attack. One evening, the first summer we were open, she stopped in to make a reservation for two for Friday night.

Fran was an attractive woman in her fifties who had total control over the millions she'd inherited. Since her deceased husband had been somewhat controlling and tight with a dollar, she was having a financially liberating experience.

Fran fancied herself something of a celebrity and possessed one of the most enormous egos and positive self-images in the tri-state area. She'd had numerous plastic surgical procedures over the years and was now availing herself to the wonders of Botox and collagen.

Whatever she was doing, it was working; she looked fabulous. She was always dressed to kill. Fran was usually overdressed for any occasion and wore extremely risqué outfits, often far too youthful for a woman her age; however, with her panache, she was usually—but not always—able to make the look work for her. She would strut in wearing her Manolos or Jimmy Choos, skin-tight designer jeans and always displaying a blouse with a plunging *décolletage*. She thought she was royalty.

At this point, my daughter Jessica was employed at Sentimento as my assistant, since my right arm was in a cast and I was still wearing a sling. The cast began below my elbow and extended to the tips of my manicured, acrylic nails, causing me to have very limited mobility.

On the evening of Fran's reservation, I personally inspected the outdoor table she had requested; it was perfectly appointed and adorned with my version of a "reserved" sign, which read *riservato*.

I was outside, chatting with a customer, when Fran and a gentleman approached me. I had heard she was dating and wasn't shocked to see her with a man; however, the gentleman she brought with her was attired as though he had lost his yacht and could not find it. He was wearing cream-colored Gucci loafers…with no socks. He had on a pair of cream-colored dress pants and a navy blazer with some sort of emblem on the pocket. Beneath the blazer, he wore a pinstriped shirt and the *pièce de résistance* was an ascot at his neck.

This man had a beautiful mane of silver hair, a very dark tan and clear nail polish on his manicured hands. His name was Phillip with two Ls, as he later informed me, and he was a realtor—however, he gave the appearance of an aging lothario.

"Here, make yourself useful. Put this on ice," he said as he attempted to toss a bottle of champagne toward me.

I immediately held up my left arm to block it and said, "Are you kidding?" I pointed to my sling. Fran intervened and introduced me to Philip with two Ls, pointing out that I was the owner and her friend. I seated them and graciously explained that I would send out a waiter with chilled champagne glasses immediately.

I didn't realize that my daughter and one of my waiters had witnessed this and were on their way to accommodate Fran and her dining companion. We always sent out an *amuse bouche*, a small, free sampling of food, to each table and in Fran's case I went back to the kitchen and had Jose "kick up the gift" by adding some extras to the plate. I carried it out to them and presented it myself.

I noticed that Nick, the waiter whose section their table was in, looked agitated. At the time, Nick was one of my premier waiters. He was always polite and rarely became flustered, and I was concerned. I inquired if something was wrong and he took me aside and blurted out, "That guy is a flaming asshole, I hate him!" I was shocked because it was out of character for Nick to react in that manner about a customer.

It was a Friday evening and I was busy stopping at each table to make sure that everything was to each customer's liking, and that there were no problems. As I walked up the long aisle toward the front, I saw Jessica, Nick and another waiter standing there, staring at something; they seemed mesmerized. I approached them to see what was going on and Jessica stood pointing toward the front door.

Fran and the illustrious Phillip with two Ls had moved their table directly in front of our glass door and, in plain view of the entire main street, removed their shoes. They were massaging each others crotches with their toes. I stood alongside my daughter and waiters, watching the porn show play out. Vincent walked up to see what was so interesting and stopped short when he realized what the content of the floorshow was.

Fran and Phillip were really into their "footsies" and apparently didn't realize or care that they were on display. When their dinner was ready, we all watched with great attentiveness as Rudolfo, a runner, served them.

Fran had been a frequent diner from the time we'd opened, so the staff was familiar with her and her demands. She was extremely high-maintenance but never mean or insulting. Phillip, on the other hand, was insulting, arrogant and spoke to Nick in such a demeaning manner, he did not want to take a dessert order or open their second bottle of wine. I sent Vincent out to open their bottle of Dolce and schmooze with them.

Vincent came back in laughing; he could not believe what a jerk this guy was. That night, they were one of the last tables to leave. They had spent the majority of the evening necking, playing crotch footsies and abusing my staff. As they departed, Phillip with two Ls winked at Fran and shouted to Vincent, "I left a huge tip for you and the boys."

Nick hurried over to see the amount. Phillip had not even left fifteen percent! Over the next few months, they were frequent diners, and Phillip almost always wore his "I've lost my yacht and can't find it" outfit. Fran often paid the bill, and they were always quite busy flagrantly necking and caressing each other's body parts. The staff enjoyed watching their weekly trysts and often had wagers on how far they would actually go. Vincent observed that her recently deceased husband, a very conservative and respected attorney, must have been spinning in his grave.

Chapter 14

The Canine Connection

I have always been an animal lover, with an emphasis on cats and dogs. Both Vincent and I grew up with pets; Vincent had dogs and I had cats and dogs. I have been the lucky recipient of love and affection from several intuitive canines and two very exceptional felines. These remarkable pets enriched my life and in many ways, shaped my life and contributed to making me the woman I am today.

A few weeks before Sentimento opened, I was up at the front of the soon-to-be restaurant when I heard a dog barking outside. One of my dogs, a ten-year-old, diabetic poodle named Cupcake, was with me and she began ripping off the paper covering the glass door in an effort to see the boisterous pooch. As she succeeded in tearing off the paper and exposing the sidewalk, I was amazed at the amount of pedestrian traffic there was on this main street and the multitude of dogs strutting right past the restaurant. It was definitely my kind of town!

The first spring and summer we were open, I was privileged to meet many of these fantastic pups and their owners. Once I realized that the same dogs passed by the restaurant every night at approximately the same time, I looked forward to seeing them and began bringing treats.

This was not an entirely altruistic gesture on my part; having a treat for them allowed me to pet them and to experience their affection. When I would spot one of my four-legged friends, I would grab my container of dog biscuits and bolt out the front door. If I was on the phone or busy, they would put their brakes on and sit down and wait outside the front door for me. If I was having a bad night, their visits never failed to cheer me up and if I was having a great evening, seeing them merely made it better.

Naturally, I had my favorites. There was Maggie, an affectionate little Bichon Frise; Buster, a personable Corgi who regularly visited nursing homes as a therapy dog; The Mighty Quinn, an Irish wolfhound who was truly a gentle giant and his partner, a beguiling young lady of mixed heritage named Corky. Clancy, an enormous Wire-Haired Terrier, would do a series of tricks in order to earn his nightly reward.

Lucy, a Golden Retriever, was eleven years old when I first made her acquaintance. The first time she sauntered up to my door, adorned in multiple strands of pearls, I knew she was special. Lucy belonged to Randall Thompson Williams III. He allowed her to approach the door unleashed and instructed her to tap on the front door to get my attention as he hid behind the mailbox. Obviously, I was surprised to see an unfamiliar pooch tapping on the glass door, adorned in pearls and unattended. I imagine I may have had a perplexed expression on my face.

Randall suddenly popped up like a jack-in-the-box and snapped my picture. He occasionally threatens to blackmail me with that photo. Although I have never seen it, I don't believe it's a flattering likeness. Lucy has since passed on, but she lived past her twelfth birthday and had a truly wonderful life. Once Randy and Dr. Mike recovered from the loss of Lucy, they adopted a two-year-old Golden Retriever named Charlie. Dr.

Mike takes him to work with him every day and Charlie reigns supreme in their lives.

A year before I sold Sentimento, Cupcake died from the ravages of old age and diabetes. She had become diabetic when she was six months old and each morning, I injected her with insulin. Her father was our dog Spike, and they were inseparable. They would run through the house together, resembling a two-headed dog.

When Spike was twelve he also developed diabetes. Each morning, I would shoot up the dogs and my diabetic in-laws; it was funny to watch them line up for their shots. Spike, a toy poodle with royal lineage, lived to the ripe old age of fourteen. He died a few years before Cupcake.

When Cupcake passed away, I was adamant that I was not getting another dog. I was so heartbroken over the loss of Spike and then Cupcake, I felt as though I just did not want to go through the pain of loss again.

Two months later, I was looking online for the perfect breeder, to find the perfect toy poodle; what I ended up with was Louie—a silver toy poodle with more issues than *Readers Digest*. He is the smartest dog I have ever owned—and the weirdest. He is anorexic and suffers from a form of irritable bowel syndrome. He has developed hypoglycemia and will pass out if I don't add liquid glucose to his diet.

Louie has his very own genuine Louis Vuitton dog carrier, a Burberry sweater and matching collar and is groomed twice a month, yet he still looks like a trash-can dog. He's a sweet little clown and very affectionate. He graduated first in his class at obedience school, but of course, that's because all the other dogs dropped out.

Spike and Cupcake appeared on Sentimento's "doggie bags"—*sachetto del cagnetto* in Italian, which literally translates to "sack of the small dog." In Italy, there is no such thing as a doggie bag.

Two months after I sold Sentimento, some of the owners of those perky Sentimento pups had a luncheon in my honor—including the dogs, of course!

One of the things I miss most since I sold the restaurant are the nightly visits from the dogs of Sentimento.

Chapter 15

Private Parties, Wine Dinners and the Christening Rumble

One of the aspects of owning a restaurant that I really detested was private parties. I usually restricted them to either Sunday afternoons or Mondays; occasionally, I would schedule one for a weekday evening. The private parties that I am referring to are large, "take over the entire restaurant" parties.

We were also the location for several wine dinners each year. The vintner would fax over a list of wines he would be presenting, with a brief synopsis of each, and we would in turn create a dish to compliment each wine. For instance, with a Cabernet Sauvignon, we might serve roasted oysters with smoked paprika sabayon and sea beans.

We once had a wine dinner and tasting where not only did a few customers become inebriated, but the vintner and sommelier presenting the night's program arrived drunk and totally incoherent! Vincent, fortunately, is quite knowledgeable when it comes to wines, having taken many wine courses over the years; however, he is not a sommelier, nor was he the vintner.

But, he took over the presentation and began to lecture the group on the type of grape used for each bottle of wine. He deftly explained the subtlety of the elusive Pinot Noir grape, the power and complexity of the super Tuscans and the vibrant structure of the dessert Rieslings. The crisis was averted and the assemblage impressed. Vincent always had a way of restoring order in the most chaotic situations and parties at the restaurant.

I always tended to refuse Communion parties since that meant multiple small children running unattended through the dining room, creating havoc. But we did have many christenings over the years.

"The Christening from Hell" was scheduled for

one o'clock p.m. on a crisp, sunny, autumn Sunday afternoon. The event was running extremely smoothly and without any major incidents. That in itself was a miracle because the parents had tormented me by constantly changing their minds about the menu, time and table arrangement.

The day was so beautiful, we decided to leave the front door open, enabling the numerous smokers to step outside for their nicotine fixes. I was approaching the smokers outside to inquire if anyone required a beverage when I heard two women screaming at each other. Standing almost nose to nose were two extremely obese women in their sixties, spewing forth vile obscenities. They were both dressed in black muumuu-dresses and stockings. The black hose they were both wearing fit neither one of them properly, causing their cankle-like ankles to have numerous rolls of adipose tissue trapped in their stockings, giving the appearance of multiple thin tourniquets wrapped around their ample legs.

As they shouted "fucking bitch," "stupid whore" and "slut" at each other, a crowd began to form in front of the restaurant. Since it was such a beautiful day, there was an abundance of pedestrian traffic outside Sentimento as well and passers-by stopped to watch the *Jerry Springer*-like show.

I approached a woman who had been introduced to me as the paternal grandmother at the christening party and suggested that she notify her son and ask him to intervene. I wanted to end the altercation before it escalated any further. She looked me in the eye and said, "Why? The one on the right is his fucking mother-in-law, the other fat bitch is her sister, and he hates both their fucking guts. He wouldn't care if they killed each other."

So much for diplomacy. The two portly women had begun pushing and swatting at each other, and the crowd viewing this was now three deep. This was not good for business. I ran to find Vincent and quickly explained the situation. Vincent said, "No problem."

He walked outside, where the dispute was taking place, and announced in a friendly yet loud voice, "Excuse me, ladies, but dinner is served!"

They immediately stopped the swatting, pushing and screaming and walked inside the restaurant, found their seats and began to chow down. End of story.

Chapter 16

Working on the Holidays

When I first thought about creating Sentimento I never really absorbed the fact that life as I knew it would never be the same. Holidays were always large celebrations in our home. On Christmas Eve, I always cooked the traditional "seven fishes," a huge *zuppa de pesce*, steamed lobsters, crab cakes, oysters, clams, mussels, eel and of course, pasta.

Our parents would usually arrive on December twenty-third and would usually stay until the twenty-seventh or twenty-eighth, even though they only lived forty-five minutes away. All of the winter holidays were celebrated in a similar manner; there were always many people, both family and friends, gathered around our dining room table. It was a huge amount of work, but I loved it.

All of our friends knew that if they didn't have any plans for a particular holiday, all they needed to do was "call Ivy" and they would instantly have an invitation. We always had large Memorial Day and Fourth of July barbecues that started in the afternoon and usually ended in the pool or hot tub in the wee hours of the morning.

I must admit, it annoyed Vinnie's mother. She simply didn't understand it and accused me of "taking in strays." She often threatened that if I kept inviting "stray" people, she would not come.

Of course, she always came; however, she would smack me on the back of my head as she walked in and call me unflattering names in Italian. Over the years, it became a game between the two of us. Her name was Giovanna but she was known as Jennie. She was a tiny little woman in stature—four feet, ten inches—yet a veritable giant in spirit. She passed away in her sleep and I still cannot believe she had the audacity to leave me, not to mention her beloved Vincent. Her last Christmas was spent with us and little did I know then that Christmas Eve would never be the same.

We worked every Christmas Eve at Sentimento after it opened, and our family would come to the restaurant and have dinner with us at the end of the dinner rush. Unbelievably, it was fun. Our "regulars" would dine with their families and we would have groups of eight, ten or more. Reservations would be made months in advance and Christmas Eve at Sentimento was very special for our customers and for us.

Vin and I never dined out on Valentine's Day; I always prepared his favorite dishes, usually tripe. Tess and Roger would usually join us, although Tess wouldn't eat tripe if her life depended on it. My daughter dreaded Valentine's Day when she was little; the second she walked in the door after school, she would shriek, "Oh no, I smell tripe! It stinks in here!" I always had to have an alternate meal for Jessica and Tess.

Since we always stayed home on Valentine's Day, I didn't realize that the rest of the free world dined out. We were only open a short time when I experienced my first Valentine's Day owning a restaurant. My restaurant could only accommodate about eighty people and even after we had turned every table twice, many people still had to be turned down. I was threatened, bribed and screamed at by individuals calling at the last minute. One would think I was denying them open-heart surgery and condemning them to a tortuous death rather than denying them a dinner reservation.

I still think of Valentine's Day as "Hell Day." In the years that followed, we did three seatings on Valentine's Day, had a price-fixed menu and were sold out weeks in advance, with a very long waiting list.

Mother's Day could also be nightmarish when I was barraged by husbands who suddenly remembered at the last minute that they had neglected to make reservations. I worked every Mother's Day, wishing other mothers a wonderful day and a fantastic dinner; however, Vincent insisted we close for Father's Day. He was adamant that Father's Day was a barbeque type of holiday and swore it was purely a business decision to close and not personal. I never believed him.

The first Valentine's Day after selling Sentimento, we went to Las Vegas to celebrate Valentine's Day along with two other couples. We stayed at the Venetian and had Valentine's dinner at Commander's Palace. Things change!

Chapter 17

Reservations, the Book and How to Choreograph the Sentimento Ballet

Our reservation book, which became known as THE BOOK, was totally controlled by me. We actually had two reservation books, one that remained at the restaurant with only the mid-week pages filled in, and then there was THE BOOK. The completed and genuine reservation book came home with me each night, since

I picked up all the messages from home beginning at nine a.m. I spent each day on the phone returning phone calls, placing orders with my purveyors and fighting with Christopher.

JoJo or another server was scheduled to arrive at the restaurant at two p.m. so that I could turn the phone duties over to them while I changed my clothes and drove to Sentimento. If they arrived by three o'clock, I was happy.

When we first opened, I allowed the experienced servers to make reservations, since they all claimed to be very knowledgeable. That lasted about ten days. I soon realized that I had inadvertently trusted idiots to do this very important part of the business. When a moronic server repeatedly made reservations for six and eight individuals at a table that could only accommodate two people, I decided it was time to severely limit their interaction with the reservation book.

I created a message book, and each request for a Friday, Saturday or holiday reservation had to be placed in the message book, hopefully with the correct phone number. I would return the call and make the reservation. On Fridays and Saturdays, I would call and confirm each reservation, alternating with confirming and picking up the messages. By nine o'clock on Saturday night, I was hoarse and could barely speak.

This cycle continued for five years. Four years into owning the restaurant, people started commenting that my voice was changing and I consulted an otolaryngologist, a throat specialist, and discovered that I had developed "singers nodes" due to voice strain. I was advised to stop speaking for ten to twelve days in order to rest my overworked vocal cords, but this was not an option. I also had a growth on my throat and that, along with my severely strained vocal cords, was causing the husky, not sultry, sound of my voice. I arranged to have surgery when we closed for vacation in January.

When you have a restaurant, it is imperative to the success of the establishment to have an efficient reservation book. It is essential that reservations be made intelligently, allowing ample time for the customer to enjoy his meal yet still giving me the ability to "flip" the table.

For example, most restaurants allow an hour and thirty minutes for two diners and two hours for four. Since I didn't have a large reception area and only had limited seating space for those waiting for their tables, I started allowing two hours for two, two hours and fifteen minutes for four and for large groups of six or more, three hours.

My main reason for extending the time allotted for dining was due to the fact that the customers waiting for their tables would become agitated and angry if they waited more than a few minutes. Since I was the main recipient of their hostility and wrath, it behooved me to have their tables ready for them. I would just hope and pray that the earlier, first-seating customers arrived at the appointed reservation time and not late; when that did occur, and it did very often, I would basically just punt and shuffle the customers around to make it work.

There were always the annoying "no shows." If you pulled a "no show" more than once, I put you on my "Nazi list," and you were never granted a weekend reservation again, or at least until I was convinced that you would actually keep it.

In order to ensure the efficiency of the restaurant, I would not make reservations in excess of four diners on Saturdays between six and nine o'clock. The reason for that is, large groups tie up tables and prevent a restaurant from flipping them; in addition, they always require additional attention from the server.

I could look at the reservation book and actually visualize the dining room in my mind's eye. Juggling the reservations to make the restaurant not only efficient but profitable as well was much like choreographing the Bolshoi Ballet.

I provided my staff with "flip times" and pertinent information on each table in their section. For instance, I let them know if there were any dietary restrictions, such as celiac disease or diabetes; if the diners were kosher or vegans; and so on. Birthdays, anniversaries and special occasions were also indicated on the flip list, which was also distributed to the kitchen staff.

There were over ninety restaurants in the Summit area, so the competition was extremely intense. Due to that fact, I soon realized that many of the no-shows were phony reservations made by other dining establishments. The bogus reservations would have been disastrous if it weren't for the benefit of caller ID.

There were also the individuals who made numerous reservations at multiple restaurants with two or three couples, who would decide at the last minute where they wanted to dine. These inconsiderate diners never bothered to cancel the numerous reservations they did not keep.

Then, there were the "tardy diners." These fools would show up whenever they felt like it. For instance, if they had an eight o'clock reservation, they might wander in at eight-fifty or nine o'clock, expecting to be seated immediately. When I would inform them that I had given their reservation away, the fireworks would begin.

During my confirmation phone calls, I always informed each prospective diner that we only held the reservation for fifteen minutes past the appointed time and then released the table to a walk-in unless notified that they were running late. "Walk-ins" are diners who do not have a pre-existing dinner reservation.

One major difficulty I experienced, which often left me feeling helpless, were diners who made reservations for six and showed up with two people; or, those who made reservations for three diners and arrived with a dining party of ten on a Saturday evening during prime time. When I would attempt to explain that I was unable to accommodate their enlarged party, the abusive language directed at me was X-rated.

An anomaly of the restaurant business is the psychotic need of "wannabe" diners to drop names in order to obtain a dinner reservation. When we first opened Sentimento, I would rarely identify myself as the owner when I answered the phone. On one Friday afternoon, I answered the phone and an agitated, arrogant woman demanded, rather than requested, a reservation for that evening.

I apologized and informed her that we had no availability, as we were totally booked until ten p.m. She then informed me that she was a personal friend of Ivy Zingara and rudely threatened to have me fired before the end of business that day. Since I *am* Ivy Zingara and did not know who she was, I did not humiliate her by identifying myself. I merely apologized again and offered to have Mrs. Zingara return her call as soon as "she" arrived. The woman called me a bitch and hung up. It was the first time a customer called me a bitch, but it certainly wasn't the last!

When you and your friends dine out in a restaurant, I'm sure you never have an inkling of the amount of hard work, diligence and planning that's behind a simple dinner reservation. The next time you dine out and there is a problem with your dinner, please remember that sometimes, things just happen, and try to be tolerant and patient.

Chapter 18

The Naughty Diner, Dirty Diapers and the Nursing Mother

Sentimento was a huge success from the moment I unlocked the front door to allow patrons to enter. As the culinary *cognoscenti* flocked to our door, we diligently tried to accommodate our customers by ensuring that our staff was competently assembled and ready to perform their duties.

I realized that a large measure of our initial success was due to the fact that we were new and the so-called flavor of the month. That, along with a sign in our front window for seven months before we opened that stated, "Coming Soon...Sentimento Ristorante," had whet the public's appetite and curiosity.

I had diligently distributed our business cards all over the county, concentrating on nail and hair salons, day spas and upscale clothing boutiques. I chose locations where women congregated since, they are usually instrumental in deciding where the dinner reservations will be made.

The discreetly placed Sentimento cards, along with numerous newspaper articles hailing the opening of the restaurant and extolling our many culinary benefits to the community, guaranteed that our tables were filled at all times. Of course, we were responsible for ensuring that they returned to Sentimento for subsequent dinners.

Our customers reveled in the luxuriously appointed restaurant as they entered the reception area. We were thrilled with the general reaction.

But there were many situations that I was not prepared for. Prior to opening Sentimento, I loved being around babies and small children; within three weeks of working at the restaurant, all maternal DNA in my body had been destroyed. I never even purchased a high chair for the restaurant. Since Sentimento was an upscale, fine dining establishment, I did not think it was necessary and did not anticipate infants, toddlers and three-year-olds as my demographic. What a surprise when parents would attempt to roll in giant strollers, sometimes two and three children wide, blocking the aisles and totally oblivious to the fact that they were not only causing chaos but violating fire laws by obstructing the aisle.

The first time a mother changed a dirty diaper on the silk settee at the entrance to the dining room, I thought I was going to have a stroke! I could not believe anyone was either that stupid or inconsiderate to change an excrement-filled, foul-smelling diaper eight feet from people attempting to enjoy their dinner. I actually had more than one mother change a diaper and leave it on the rug next to the podium and authoritatively state to me, "Take care of this—my dinner is getting cold."

About one month after opening Sentimento, I had a sign printed—"Please...No strollers or carriages... Thank you!"—and placed it on the front door for all to see. I actually secretly longed to place a baby's photograph in a circle with a diagonal line going through it on the front door. Sentimento was not what one would describe as a "child friendly" restaurant. I refused to ever purchase a high chair or booster seat and went out of my way to inform potential patrons of this fact.

There were many incidents when adult customers requested I relocate them to another table on a busy Saturday night due to an ill-mannered child sitting near them or a screaming baby in an infant seat disturbing them. When my children were babies, they did not accompany us on a Saturday evening as we dined with friends; if we could not obtain the services of a competent baby-sitter, we stayed home.

Things seem to have changed, as the age of first-time parents appears to be getting older and older due to the advances of modern medicine. I observed over the years that first-time parents in their forties seemed oblivious to the fact that their screaming toddler might be annoying anyone or that allowing a five-year-old child to butter a chair in a restaurant was unacceptable behavior.

I once had a six-year-old take a dish of linguini and smear it all over the stucco wall; I waited a minute before I approached the table, assuming that surely, his parents would reprimand him. When they ignored the situation entirely, I approached the table and said, "Don't you like your pasta? Would you like me to bring you something else to eat?"

I did not really intend to bring him an alternative meal to smear on the wall but thought that by making the offer, I would not appear hostile, which of course I was.

His mother informed me, "He is merely expressing himself." She said that as he continued to use the linguini as finger paint and the wall as his canvas.

I witnessed two ten-year-old boys start a fire at a table; while their parents chatted, they ignited a napkin.

The parents were annoyed when I poured water on the flaming napkin, and then they failed to discipline the offending youths.

In almost all of these situations, in my opinion, it was the parents' fault since the children were obviously unaccustomed to any form of discipline or had never been taught acceptable parameters of behavior.

In all fairness, I must state that we had some customers who had absolutely charming and well behaved children whose presence we not only enjoyed, but also looked forward to. When an eight-year-old girl politely asks, "May I please have extra capers on the bronzini?"—you have to love it!

I once informed a couple that we did not allow strollers or carriages in the restaurant and pointed to the large sign on the front door; I was not rude, I merely stated a fact. The father reacted in an angry manner—he picked up the baby, handed the toddler to his wife and then repeatedly smashed the stroller on the ceramic tile floor until he cracked a tile. I stood there watching this jerk whack the stroller on the floor until he realized he had accomplished his goal of damaging the floor, at which time he said, "Fuck you! Have a nice day!"

He said that with a broad smile on his face as he triumphantly slammed the stroller against the wall. After his departure, I remained at the podium in a state of shock; I could not believe what I had just witnessed. The man had actually frightened me and I was relieved that he'd whacked and slammed the stroller on the tile instead of on me!

I understand the plight of the nursing mother. I once *was* a nursing mother; however, I was discreet about it. There are methods and positions in which to nurse a baby that prevent onlookers from realizing what you are doing; I know this because I was very adept at this technique. Any woman who has ever nursed a baby, in public or private, will tell you it is not necessary to flamboyantly expose both breasts while feeding your infant; I must admit that I never actually whipped out a breast in public.

We once had a nursing mother who, by the way, was not even dining in my restaurant, but who chose to walk up and down the serving aisle with both breasts exposed during the dinner rush. Initially, we were reluctant to say anything to her, fearful of a scene and/or litigation, since nursing mothers have rights, as they should. Vincent, the coward, refused to say or do anything; he instructed me to inform her she was blocking the aisle as he disappeared into the kitchen.

I approached her and inquired if she would be more comfortable sitting. I offered her either a chair or the use of the silk settee up front. I even offered to provide a stool to elevate and rest her feet. She thought about it and reluctantly positioned herself on the settee as she exposed both breasts and flashed each patron as they entered Sentimento. She seemed happy and comfy; the gentlemen entering or exiting the dining room seemed to enjoy the situation, as did my waiters.

When she finished nursing the baby, she reluctantly put herself back together and left; obviously, she was not your usual nursing mother. Although she was not a customer, she did provide a certain degree of entertainment for my customers that evening.

Individuals dining out expect, and rightfully so, to be treated with respect and spoken to in a polite manner. However, many diners speak to waiters and other staff as though they are subservient, second-class citizens. They are rude and abusive. The public expects to be treated in a courteous manner but they should understand that proper etiquette should also be extended the person about to take their dinner orders.

We experienced our share of babies, name-droppers, no-shows, late diners, dining rubes and wannabes. We learned how to handle them politely and efficiently, without ever offending them. I often wished that there were some type of behavior code or rulebook for diners; it would be very short. The main rules would be:

1. Do not abuse the staff.
2. Do not annoy your fellow diners.
3. Curtail loud cell phone activity at the table.
4. Do not bring babies and small children to

restaurants that are unable to accommodate them.

5. Do not punish your waiter if you don't enjoy the food. If he has been helpful, give him a fair tip. Don't shoot the messenger, but make sure that the server knows you are displeased so that the owner has the opportunity to make amends.

Restaurateurs want to make your dining experience at their establishments enjoyable diversions. The owners want you to have excellent service; they try to execute the meal properly and efficiently and want you to return again another day.

A restaurant succeeds only if there is repeat business and positive word-of-mouth endorsements. The one thing they want most of all is for you to spread the word and tell your friends how much you enjoyed your dining experience.

Unbelievably, there are no restaurateurs who want their customers to have an unpleasant dining experience in their establishment. Unfortunately, sometimes things go wrong due to circumstances beyond their control.

Chapter 19

The Wine Slut

My husband Vincent is a devout oenophile. He loves wine and everything remotely related to wine. He is a graduate of the Windows on the World Wine School and is a Kevin Zraly devotee. He loves to discuss wine, study the varied components that affect the flavor of the wine and all things pertaining to the successful execution of a delicious vintage. He enjoys learning about the grapes, the pH of the soil in which they are grown, the optimum aging of the wine and the proper storage environment required to ensure the wine's stability.

He spends endless hours in his own temperature-controlled, environmentally correct, moisture-efficient wine cellar. Vincent is a perfectionist and becomes obsessive-compulsive when it comes to his wine and cellar. All the bottles are segregated geographically by country and region. Each bottle is individually tagged with its vintage and approximate maturity so that, as Orson Welles was famous for saying, "No wine will be drunk before its time."

A few years before I created Sentimento, Vincent insisted we attend the Monterey Wine Festival in California. I have rarely seen him that enthused about anything; he reminded me of a small boy about to be granted *carte blanche* at FAO Schwartz! He appeared intoxicated with anticipation at the mere thought of spending five days imbibing the best wines California had to offer. Although I was looking forward to the upcoming events, I did not share his enthusiasm—nor did I possess his fervor, that of a crazed wine zealot!

The opening night event was the champagne testing, held at an incredibly fabulous aquarium. The walls were ceiling-to-floor glass so that we could view the aquarium's inhabitants as we strolled from one champagne station to another. The ambiance of the location and the excitement of the event were thrilling; we were having a wonderful time when Vincent observed that there were no visible spit buckets.

In case you have never attended a wine or champagne tasting, the key word is *tasting*. When you attend one of these events, usually, you are given a small amount to taste and at each "station," there is usually a "spit bucket"—which is exactly what it sounds like. You spit the excess wine in it.

Vincent immediately warned me, stating, "You better be careful—you know you have a low tolerance for alcohol. Until I find a spit bucket, stop drinking!"

"I am fine! I can handle it," I said, ignoring his warning.

He did not appear to believe me and took off in a hurry to attempt to find the elusive spit buckets. When he returned, he informed me that there were no spit buckets provided at this event. This was not good news for me, since the numerous champagnes I had already "tasted" seemed to be affecting me already.

Vincent observed the change in my demeanor and did not seem pleased. He was very anxious to continue the tasting experience and appeared determined not to allow my inability to effectively metabolize alcohol ruin the evening for him.

I encouraged him to continue without me; he propped me up against a glass wall—not only were there no spit buckets, but there were also no chairs—and said, "I'll be back soon."

The room seemed to be swirling as I developed a case of the "whirlies." I glanced to my right and noticed that he had leaned me up against the shark tank. No problem—after all, I was protected by the glass. I soon realized I was providing entertainment not only for the sharks, but also for the attendees of the event who happened to stroll past the shark tank.

When Vincent returned, he thought it was one of the more amusing sights he had witnessed and regretted not having a camera present. Unbeknownst to me, it seems that the sharks began swarming around in a group on the other side of the glass wall, while slightly inebriated patrons stood and gaped at the sight.

I have related this event in an attempt to demonstrate how much Vinnie loves the entire wine experience. After all, he did not actually feed me to the sharks; he merely leaned me up against the glass as though I were the *hors d'oeuvre du jour.*

The one thing that Vincent loves most about wine, not surprisingly, is drinking it. He loves to swirl the wine in a Reidel crystal glass in order to observe its "legs," color and aroma. He enjoys handing me a glass of wine, instructing me to close my eyes and relate what I taste. Vincent will say, "Do you taste the wood? What does it taste like to you?"

I usually disappoint him, but he never gives up the quest and continues to attempt to educate my palate.

Sentimento, which was located in New Jersey, did not possess a liquor license. Although we were unable to sell alcohol, we were legally allowed to permit our customers to bring their own wine, beer or champagne to our establishment. Our patrons, many of whom were oenophiles, were thrilled to learn that we provided excellent German crystal wine glasses, and were willing and able to decant their wine into crystal decanters.

We were open only a few weeks when I observed that when a customer came to Sentimento carrying an exceptional wine, Vincent's eyes would light up! He would always manage to bolt over to the table, before the server, and deftly open the wine, offer to decant it, all the while commenting on the grape, the vineyard and vintage—all in an effort to be offered a taste of the nectar of the gods. I found his antics to be amusing at first and eventually realized that our customers were actually bringing special wines for Vin to ooh and ahh over, and to perform his commentary while sharing a glass with them.

We actually had large groups of wine devotees having monthly wine dinners at Sentimento. I had no idea there were so many affluent wine groups in the area and when they called, they always asked for Vincent. They would then inform him of the number of courses required, the wines they intended to bring and if a speaker or vintner would be attending the dinner. As soon as we knew the exact year and vintage of the wine, Vincent would look it up and actually obtain a profile and review; this enabled us to match the wine to food that would compliment the vintage.

The wine dinners usually occurred on Monday evenings, when Sentimento was closed to the public. Over the years, we hosted some fantastic wine events; we met famous vintners, whom we were honored to serve. We even hosted several vertical tastings and had the pleasure of hosting a barrel tasting.

Vincent was always very exuberant concerning an impending wine dinner and the élan and fervor he displayed during these events absolutely thrilled the clientele.

While I handled the dining room, checked on the kitchen shenanigans and even cleaned the bathrooms during the course of an evening, my charming husband would glide through the dining room, pausing to chat with customers while carrying an empty wine glass. The participants of this captive audience loved it! They would call him over to their tables to taste their evening's wine choice, and of course, he always complied with their requests.

One evening, our friend Anthony and his wife were having dinner at Sentimento. When the dinner rush quieted down, I went over to chat with them and sat down at their table. Anthony laughed and shook his head as he pointed to Vinnie.

The three of us watched as the love of my life worked the room "like a hooker in a room full of sailors," to use one of my dad's favorite expressions. Vinnie's goal that particular night was to be offered a taste of a Chateau Petrus. Anthony and I were wagering on whether or not he would succeed. I bet against Vincent and Anthony wagered that he would be granted a taste. Anthony won the bet.

Vincent schmoozed and charmed the customers as he sauntered through the dining room until he stopped at Anthony's table and sat down. He was so pleased with himself. I looked at him and said, "You are such a slut when it comes to wine. Get a grip."

Vincent replied, "Maybe you're right, but I'm holding a glass of Petrus and you're not!" He finished the Petrus without even offering me a sip.

Chapter 20

Panic in the Pantry

Once upon a Monday morning, I arrived early at Sentimento to update the inventory. While I waited for my coffee to brew, I thought I heard a noise emanating from the rear of the restaurant. I walked in, surveyed the area and neither seeing nor hearing anything awry, forgot about it.

The area Vinnie and I used for our office was located in the basement of the restaurant. I carried my coffee and my briefcase down to the bowels of Sentimento to start the *project du jour*, and I heard the noise again. I started looking around but I did not hear or see anything unusual.

In general, I am exceedingly uncomfortable in basements. Actually, I have been positively terrified of basements since childhood, due to an unfortunate incident. I will not enter ours at home after dark without Vincent accompanying me.

I turned on the radio in order to create a pleasant, melodic background and attempted to dismiss the fact that I had heard anything. I thought I was just being paranoid and refused to allow an old childhood fear dominate my actions.

About four hours later, as I neared completion of the task I was working on, I went to check the back-up inventory in the metal pantry. The pantry was utilized for storing replacement items and dry goods such as imported teas, legumes, rice, dried herbs and the like. The pantry was about six feet high and eight feet wide and had double side-by-side doors. It was supposed to be closed and locked at all times.

As I approached the pantry, I noticed someone had left the doors open—again. Initially, I feared that one of my trusty employees had decided to go grocery shopping in my pantry. The reason I insisted that Christopher keep it locked at all times was due to employee pilfering. When I looked inside, it appeared that nothing was missing, and I was shocked and pleased simultaneously.

I noticed that two of the four stainless steel drawers were slightly ajar and as I went to adjust them, I heard something move; thinking it was a rolling jar of herbs, I opened the drawer. Surprise! It was not rolling jars of herbs. It was three   yes, three!—baby possums!

I stood there aghast for a few seconds as this bizarre and inappropriate sight registered in my mind. I had no idea where Mama Possum was but I am still extremely grateful she was nowhere in the vicinity when I opened the drawer.

If you have ever seen a possum close up, you are aware that they are not cute or cuddly. They do not inspire the desire in one to attempt to adopt, feed or pet them. Conversely, they may even inspire repulsion, disgust and in my case, fear! They possess beady little black eyes, matted, beige and black fur, razor-sharp rows of teeth and a rodent-like tail. An adult possum also has a strange gait.

That previous winter had been extremely cold and the area had endured several blizzards. Due to these meteorological conditions, according to the exterminator I hired at my home that winter, these nocturnal, rat-like creatures kept visiting my deck each night. The exterminator, who specialized in wildlife capture, promised to catch and relocate the wayward possum family.

He set up "harm-free, creature friendly" cages on and under my deck, on the three levels of patios and in my courtyard. The lure in each cage was peanut butter; the possums were uninterested and unimpressed by it.

Since my only night off was Monday, when Sentimento was closed, I only cooked on Mondays. We had an elaborate Weber grill on the deck, which I used year-round. When it snowed we merely shoveled a path from the French doors to the grill.

That winter, every Monday night, when I would attempt to use the grill, one or more possums would climb onto the deck and cause me to go running into the house screaming. We tried blocking the gates with chicken wire and two-by-fours, all to no avail. I began keeping a shovel and a broom on the deck in order to defend myself if need be.

One night, the dogs followed me out onto the deck as I was lighting the grill. Right on cue, two possums appeared. The poodles started yapping, and I began shrieking. I grabbed the pups, threw the shovel at the trespassing possums and bolted into the safety of my kitchen.

They appeared to enjoy the fact that they were tormenting me; as we would have dinner, they would actually line up in front of the ceiling-to-floor windows and peer in at us as we ate. I HATE OPOSSUMS.

Now, to behold three of them in my restaurant, in the basement that I already feared, instilled terror, loathing and total panic in my mind. I bolted up the stairs, shrieking from the basement to the kitchen. I quickly slammed the door behind me and realized I had left my purse, keys and coat down in the basement.

I immediately called Vincent at his office, babbling hysterically. When he finally deciphered what I was attempting to relate, he started laughing—not exactly the response I was looking for. I calmed down and called the exterminator we used at the restaurant. I must have been persuasive because within fifteen minutes, a licensed and certified exterminator appeared; about ten minutes later, Vincent arrived. By this time, the offending creatures were no longer napping in the pantry but scampering around the basement, with the exterminator in hot pursuit. Vincent retrieved my belongings and suggested I leave. I made a hasty retreat.

Vincent said that after two hours, the exterminator gave up and called in a "possum expert." The next morning, I received a panicked call from Christopher, stating, "There are fucking possums all over the place!"

He called me from his cell phone outside Sentimento. "I'm freezing my ass off," he screamed. "It's four fucking degrees out here and I don't have my coat! Do something and do it now!"

I explained what had transpired the previous day and informed him that the possum expert was on his way, as was Vincent. I decided to join them at the "possum party" and drove to Sentimento wearing my jeans, a sweatshirt, sneakers *sans* make-up.

It is difficult to verbally paint a picture of the slapstick comedy that transpired over the next few hours, but just close your eyes and imagine the Three Stooges chasing possums. They chased those little varmints up the stairs, through the kitchen, back down the stairs and into corners and each and every time, those crafty little critters escaped successfully. After a few more hours, it was imperative that I leave the premises, go home, change my clothes and prepare for the dinner rush. I just hoped and prayed that those elusive marsupials would keep a low profile all evening.

That night, although we were very busy, we experienced no unwelcomed dinner guests in the form of our furry squatters. Around eleven-thirty p.m., as I was straightening out the dining room, I heard a ruckus out back. The waiters, runners, busboys, chefs and line cooks were all yelling and laughing as they surrounded someone whom I could not identify due to the manner in which they had him encompassed. I saw Vincent out there also, clapping and laughing; even Christopher seemed genuinely thrilled about something.

Enquiring minds and short people, such as myself, needed to know what the heck was going on. I pushed my way through the throng of employees only to discover an extremely gory sight. Standing in the center of the crowd, a conquering gladiator of sorts stood erect and proud: Luiz, the dishwasher, had somehow managed to skewer onto a pitchfork all three offending furry foraging trespassers!

It was not the conclusion I would have chosen for them; I guess I would have preferred them to be frolicking in the woods far, far away. I still can't figure out how the three intruders gained access to Sentimento or my pantry or for that matter, how the pitchfork miraculously appeared. However, it did provide closure and remove the possums from the pantry for ever!

Chapter 21

Presenting
Mr. Bernie
Greenblatt

One of the more successful dining establishments in our area was a French restaurant called Armand's, appropriately named after the owner, Armand Dumaine. It was located in a beautiful restored mansion in a genteel section of town. The impressive estate featured a winding driveway embellished with beautiful landscaping.

The owner and chef, Armand, had been working in Louisiana for several years as a sommelier/chef and his publicist was busy bombarding the local newspapers, touting his new restaurant. The foodies anxiously awaited the opening of Armand's.

Armand Dumaine opened his restaurant several months before Sentimento, so needless to say, I was extremely busy and did not pay much attention to the hoopla surrounding his unveiling. Approximately two months before we opened Sentimento, Tess, Roger, Vin and I made a reservation to dine at Armand's. I was informed by a cold and haughty female voice that she required my American Express numbers in order to secure the reservation; I complied. She then informed me that failure to keep the reservation for four would result in a charge of one hundred dollars, and that a forty-eight hour notice was required for a cancellation— no exceptions. I assured her we would be there.

On Saturday evening, we entered the charming restaurant on time and were escorted to our table. A few minutes later, a well dressed gentleman inquired if we desired a cocktail, which we did. We placed our beverage order with the gentlemen and he promptly disappeared.

Twenty minutes later, someone else delivered two cosmos and a martini; however, Roger's Harvey's Bristol Cream was deleted. Eventually, we were presented a wine list and menus; Roger kept inquiring about his missing drink, to no avail.

We ordered our dinner and wine and still, poor Roger's drink was MIA. He was becoming cranky as Tess and I teased him. We were enjoying our second glass of wine when someone eventually appeared with Roger's Harvey's. Roger no longer desired the long-tardy liquor and attempted to send it back along with an explanation.

He was informed by an arrogant and rude gentleman that he didn't have to drink it if he so desired; however, it would remain on the bill. He made that statement with a phony smile plastered on his face and his final remark to us was, "Enjoy!"

The gourmet meal was delicious but minute; the servings were miniature replicas of an actual portion, and the price was stellar. Dinner for the four of us came to seven hundred eighty-nine dollars! The worst aspect of the meal, other than the price, was that everyone was still hungry. We exited Armand's and drove directly to our house, where I immediately prepared a small feast to calm growling tummies and empty wallets.

A few months after Sentimento opened, Armand Dumaine called to make a reservation for a Thursday evening at nine o'clock. When he entered Sentimento, he was carrying a large case; he had brought along his own wine glasses, not trusting ours.

Vincent was his usual gallant self. He seated Armand and opened the wine, pouring it into his glasses as a busboy adeptly removed ours from the table. I immediately went into the kitchen to inform Christopher that Armand was in the house. I gave him Armand's location as I prepared a special *amuse bouche*.

I instructed Nick to be his server and alerted the rest of the staff to be on their toes, assigning the most professional busboy to the table.

It was a very busy evening and even at nine-thirty, we still had a full house; this fact, although it pleased me, seemed to distress Armand. I made sure he received "VIP RED CARPET" treatment and was actually proud of my staff and the job they were doing. Armand did not seem very happy as he realized that we shared many of the same customers. He actually got up from his seat and started working the room!

I wasn't alarmed or concerned at first, but then I realized he was making my customers uncomfortable, and that was unacceptable. I graciously approached the grandiose egomaniac known as Armand and escorted him back to his seat, informing him that his dinner was about to be served. His face turned scarlet as he returned to his table, having abandoned his significant other for a prolonged period of time.

I returned to the kitchen to ensure the presentation

and integrity of the dishes and the entire kitchen staff started clapping. This was a shocker, since I had no idea why I was being given the accolade.

It seems that Mr. Armand Dumaine, owner of the extremely expensive and exclusive Armand's, was actually Mr. Bernie Greenblatt, formerly of Marlton, New Jersey. As luck would have it, my pasta chef had worked with Armand, a.k.a. Bernie, at a restaurant in Philadelphia a few years earlier. The presently sophisticated and nattily attired Armand, with his oversized Windsor-knotted Dolce and Gabbana tie, enormous ego and supercilious ways, was about to have his true identity revealed! In reality, he was obnoxious Bernie Greenblatt, the former waiter best known for his expertise at kissing up to his superiors with gratuitous compliments.

Mr. Bernard Greenblatt had successfully and totally reinvented himself. Obviously, he did not count on being recognized by Robby, the pasta chef. When Robby walked out of the kitchen and approached the waiters' station in the rear of the restaurant, Armand, a.k.a. Bernie, happened to glance in his direction and not only saw Robby, but obviously recognized him. He appeared visibly shaken; his entire demeanor suddenly altered and the color drained from his cheeks.

Armand's dining companion was oblivious to the situation, as he continued to enjoy his dinner. Robby never approached his old co-worker Bernie; he merely stood there with his arms folded in front of his chest and stared directly at him, smirking.

Mr. Armand Dumaine, formerly known as Mr. Bernie Greenblatt, never dined at Sentimento again.

Chapter 22

Crisis du Jour and the Saga of the Barrel Fuse

There was always a crisis or some sort of daily drama at Sentimento. Usually, it was not catastrophic, but occasionally, it caused my heart to skip a beat or two—not quite ventricular tachycardia or atrial fibrillation, but close enough.

Usually, the crisis *du jour* was annoying and could be rectified; however, every so often, my ability to correct the crisis was challenged.

The first tale began one Saturday night in August of 2003. On that extremely hot Saturday evening, we were totally booked; we had customers waiting for tables both inside the restaurant and outdoors, even though it was over ninety-five degrees.

The five o'clock diners had departed and the entire dining room was full when half the lights in the dining room went dark. Vince ran to the basement to check the electrical box while I assured customers I had everything under control.

As I went from table to table, I realized that the air conditioning was no longer functioning. I was nearly paralyzed with fear at the mere thought of a malfunctioning air conditioner but more importantly, at the loss of electricity. Please keep in mind that this incident occurred the Saturday after New York City experienced a blackout due to a grid problem in the northeast quadrant or something like that, so my fears were well founded.

When we discovered we were the only establishment on our street affected, I immediately called one of our despicable landlords and received a recording that he was vacationing on the Riviera and would not be returning until September. I immediately made a thorough and expeditious attempt to locate a repairman.

Vincent started calling electricians, but to no avail; after the tenth call, he decided to call Salvatore, the owner of a business down the street, for assistance.

Salvatore had remarkable resources at his fingertips. He made one phone call and ten minutes later, an electrician magically appeared in front of my podium, carrying his toolbox. The entire dining room started clapping and actually gave him a standing ovation!

My customers were fantastic that night. I was busy going from table to table, apologizing to my diners, when the lights and air-conditioning went back on and my dining room erupted in applause and laughter.

Before the repair occurred, the kitchen was as panic-stricken as I was. The refrigerators, freezers, stoves, oven and computer systems were functioning; however, the ventilation unit was not, nor was the air conditioning or the giant exhaust fans in the kitchen. The temperature rose rapidly to over one hundred fifteen degrees!

During the power outage, I was in and out of the kitchen, constantly checking to see if they were able to continue serving meals and as a result of this, I was soaked with perspiration. The temperature in the dining room only rose to eighty degrees for a short time but the kitchen felt as though you were walking into hell, complete with flames.

That night, almost every customer was wonderful, with the exception of two women I knew—one in particular happened to be a neighbor of mine. They were part of a group of six and actually came in an hour after the chaos had ended and the problem had been repaired; however, they overheard everyone talking about it.

One of my waiters approached me and informed me that a woman at table seven was causing a commotion and was behaving very rudely to him. I knew immediately who it was, even before he identified the table number. My high-maintenance and obnoxious neighbor Ava was busy pontificating to her entire entourage, informing them that they should leave immediately because I was probably going to poison them with warm, bacteria-laden food.

I took a deep breath, wiped the sweat off my brow, plastered a faux smile across my moist face and walked over to their table. She began to speak to me in an extremely demeaning manner before I could even utter a sound. I let her go on and state her fears for a few minutes; I then inquired if she was finished.

She eventually nodded and I addressed the table, appearing relaxed and smiling as I explained what was affected by the partial power outage. I informed them that the refrigeration was not impacted; however, if they felt unsure and wished to leave, I would certainly understand. I went on to assure them that I would never put myself or my customers' health in jeopardy by serving food that was not properly stored—and then walked away, still smiling.

Ava was the variety of customer that all restaurateurs dreaded. She was impossible to satisfy; she complained about everything from the moment she entered the establishment. I usually had to change the location of her table two to three times before she settled in for the evening. Once she was satisfied with the location, she would usually force the diners in her party to switch seats with her due to either an imaginary draft, the fact that she would experience an anxiety attack and hyperventilate if forced to face a wall, and on and on.

Regardless of what item she would order, invariably, it was always sent back to the kitchen. Sometimes, it was because she forgot to tell the server that she was allergic to something or that she changed her mind and wanted another appetizer or entrée. When this occurred, Christopher would go totally nuclear. He would start throwing things, threatening the server and cursing at me as though the whole thing were my fault. Ava complained constantly, yet week after week, she returned to dine at Sentimento.

When the drama began that night, I made the mistake of not removing my suit jacket; beneath my Dana Buchman jacket was a sweat-soaked silk camisole that was literally stuck to my skin. I wanted to remove my jacket more than I can say but kept it on because of the giant wet splotches in the front and back of the camisole. My hair was dripping around my face and I was doing my best to assure that my diners were taken care of.

I returned to the podium to answer the phone when one of the men who had been sitting at Ava's table came up to me and apologized for Ava's rude and inappropriate behavior. To this day, I feel grateful for his kind words and thank him repeatedly every time I see him.

The problem that caused the power outage turned out to be a burnt-out barrel fuse, thus the evening became known as the "saga of the barrel fuse." For several months after that hot and sultry Saturday evening, I kept the ancient barrel fuse on my desk at home as a reminder that you never know what will happen next at Sentimento!

Another memorable Saturday began with an offensive phone call from one of our penny-pinching landlords at eight in the morning. He was screaming at me that we had caused a gas leak and threatening me with several different scenarios if I did not fix it immediately.

We contacted the gas company and Vince bolted over to Sentimento. The gas company thought the leak was in front of the building, under the sidewalk, directly in front of our door. The fire department was summoned and the entire street was closed off as they began to dig up the cobblestone and pavers that comprised our decorative sidewalk and *al fresco* dining area.

This digging started at ten a.m. and continued until three forty-five in the afternoon. During the minor construction, the authorities would not allow any employees into the building to prep for the Saturday evening dinner rush and we didn't know if we would open for that evening. We were stuck in restaurant limbo, at the mercy of the fire department and the gas company.

After the gas company destroyed the entire area in front of our restaurant, they announced it was a false alarm and there was no leak, and left after explaining that they were not responsible for closing up the hole or repairing the damage; it would be my responsibility.

At four o'clock, they re-opened the street and allowed my employees to enter the building through the back, and that was when we discovered they had not turned the gas back on. We had to wait for "the guy who turns the gas back on," but we still had the problem of the destroyed sidewalk and the fact that it was impossible to enter through the front entrance.

Vincent thought we should just cancel all the reservations for Saturday evening and Sunday. Since we were closed on Monday, he said he would have it repaired then.

"No way!" I declared.

Vincent attempted to convince me that I was being irrational and unrealistic. I ignored him and followed my own instinct. I remembered a customer who was a mason, who had given me his business card; I called him immediately. Miraculously, he answered the phone!

Unfortunately, he informed me that he and his brother were on their way to go fishing and he couldn't help me. I begged and pleaded and groveled in an attempt to change his mind. It worked! He said I sounded so desperate and pathetic, he would do it.

Once that obstacle was resolved I gathered every pot I owned and drove them to the restaurant in an effort to aid the kitchen staff in the evening's prepping. Our giant pots would take too long to heat, so I brought every piece of Farberware I had to Sentimento.

I am proud to say we opened for dinner promptly at five o'clock, had our outdoor dining area perfectly arranged and had one of our busiest Saturday nights of that summer. Another near catastrophe averted!

There were many near-disasters over the years; however, there was one that repeatedly occurred, with compliments of Christopher.

Some days he would come to work with a bad attitude and a "bug up his ass," looking for a fight with someone. When I say "fight," I don't mean anything physical, as in punching or hitting—just a verbal altercation with some flying pots and pans. Saturdays and holidays were no exception.

It was a very busy March evening, and we happily had a full house, as usual. Lorenzo, who eventually bought Sentimento from us, entered the restaurant for dinner. He had arranged for someone else to call for the reservation with a different name, and I had unknowingly given him a reservation. When he entered, I did not know who he was, as I had never met him and refused to speak with him when he called with his many offers. However, Vincent had met him, and introduced us.

I wanted to kick my own ass for giving Lorenzo the reservation and admittedly was taken aback by the situation. Vincent seated him as I tried to compose myself, since

I really didn't want him in MY restaurant. His lies had caused me difficulties in the past.

The phone rang and the caller ID revealed that it was Christopher, calling on the cell phone I paid for. He began a foul, vicious and depraved verbal assault of obscenity, directed at me. He informed me that if I did not kick Lorenzo out of the restaurant immediately, the entire kitchen staff would walk out and never return.

It was nine-thirty and there wasn't an empty seat; we were on our third seating of the evening. I handed the phone to Vincent, and Christopher ranted and raved at him. Eventually, Vincent convinced the miscreant of the error of his ways, and of the possible repercussions of such an action, including legal ramifications.

Christopher reluctantly returned to his post in the kitchen, but before returning, felt the need to call again from the cell phone to relay the following message to me: "Eat shit and die, Ivy, you fuck-faced ugly bitch!" Nothing out of the ordinary.

Another disaster averted. The evening progressed as normal and none of the customers were aware of the situation. At the end of the evening, we called an employee meeting in the dining room to explain that these types of threats and tactics were unacceptable and would not be tolerated.

Christopher refused to attend and stormed out of the building. He did not show up for work the next day, although he returned on Tuesday as if nothing had happened. He even called me at home to chat in a friendly manner about the specials for the evening. I followed his lead and did not mention the Saturday night drama.

Christopher's inappropriate and malicious behavior that evening convinced Vincent that we should sell Sentimento. I refused, and thus began the six month "Sentimento War" between my husband and myself.

Chapter 23

Wild Game, Tripe, Cow Lips and River Rat

The first winter we were open, there was a tremendous amount of snowstorms. Not blizzards—just a lot of snow and inconvenience, including difficulty finding adequate parking. We were concerned as to the possible impact it would have on our business when Vince came up with the idea of "Wild Game Month"!

Prior to creating Sentimento, we had attended the Kentucky Derby with friends. Each year, we would dine at our favorite restaurant in Louisville; their specialty was wild game. Ostrich, boar, elk, venison and an array of game fowl were always on the menu, as well as some items I thought were against the law to kill or eat.

We were discussing the Derby when Vincent remembered the delicious game we enjoyed in Louisville, and so "Wild Game Month" was created.

We immediately began contacting every purveyor who specialized in wild game and planning the menu and advertising. The response was overwhelming! Our diners came out in rain, snow or sleet to gobble up our game. The thought of rabbit cacciatore, ostrich Milanese, beer-braised buffalo short ribs and venison Bolognese filled our dining room with a new demographic of customers: the "game foodies." We were not aware that they existed in such huge numbers and were absolutely thrilled with the positive response.

Many of these game foodies were hunters and began requesting everything from elk, bear and alligator to African river rat. One of our customers, a retired, elderly yet robust millionaire, enjoyed participating in African safaris, which was where he first dined on African river rat. He claimed it was the most delectable meat he had ever dined on and constantly urged us to add it to our menu. We declined. Another customer requested cow lips and beef cheeks, but I did not consider cow lips to be wild game—they were merely repulsive.

As a small child, I'd enjoyed tongue sandwiches until I'd gone to the deli with my father one Sunday morning. My father had ordered one pound of tongue and the counterman had said, "Coming right up."

He'd walked into the back room and come out carrying what appeared to be an enormous cow's tongue. It was then that I'd realized that the tongue I'd enjoyed with Kosciusko mustard was in reality a cow's tongue. I never ate it again; the sight of that giant tongue, which really looked like a tongue, left a lasting impression.

I do not have a problem with tripe or sweetbreads; however, cow lips, boar snout and any animal's sautéed testicles, be it boar or lamb, still repulses me.

We had a group of wealthy Italians who longed for tripe since their wives refused to ever consider preparing it. Every time we put it on the menu, I would fax them at work to inform them that it was "*trippa* night." We would serve it in a heavy red sauce in a bowl, just the way Vinnie's Aunt Yolanda had meticulously instructed me.

Our friend Ciro, an amazing and talented chef, keeps tripe on his menu twelve months a year. People come from all over New Jersey just to sample his tripe and his delicious comfort food. He has a loyal and

devoted staff because he believes in treating his employees with respect and consideration—something that
Christopher never learned.

Chapter 24

Botox for Bolognese

My restaurant was prominently known and famous for our Bolognese sauce. It was a thick and rich sauce made with ground pork, veal and beef, prepared in the style of Emilia-Romagna. This part of Italy totally fascinates me and I am very captivated by its charm.

Emilia-Romagna is a region in Italy located near the Apennine Mountains, the Adriatic Sea and the Po River.

This region of Italy acquired its distinctive name due to the fact that the Romans created a strategically important road in order to increase trade, called via Emilia. This road extended from the western town of Piacenza to the eastern town of Rimini, thus the region became named Emilia-Romagna.

Sentimento was not merely an Italian restaurant but a regional Italian restaurant. We prepared dishes from all over Italy and Sicily. In August, we usually did a week specializing in recipes from Emilia-Romagna; in September, we usually featured delicacies that originated in the region of Tuscany. We attempted to give our patrons a culinary tour of Italy by tempting their palates with superb entrees from every region.

Different regions in Italy are known for certain specialties. For instance, Campania is known for mozzarella di buffalo, the most cherished of the fresh mozzarellas; Piedmont is known for its basil; and so on.

I think what makes the region of Emilia-Romagna so unique is not its geographical beauty or the fantastic cuisine, but the enchanting and friendly people who populate the region. I openly admit to being bewitched, captivated and enamored by that region of Italy.

The customers of Sentimento went wild for my Bolognese recipe and word spread quickly. At first, the recipe was my creation; however, over time, Christopher attempted to bastardize my rendition by adding or deleting necessary ingredients and in the end, it was no longer MY recipe.

I was and am very proud of MY Bolognese recipe. I perfected it over many years and it was one of my father-in-law's favorite dishes. He also loved the way I prepared tripe; he used to say, "It tastes just lika my mama's! Are you sure you're not from Calabria?" For me, it was the ultimate compliment.

I have a very close friend, Karl, a renowned plastic surgeon who absolutely adores my Bolognese. In fact, he may have developed a severe addiction problem to its rich sauce. Whenever he dined at Sentimento, which was quite often, I always sent out a platter of penne Bolognese to his table as a gift. Karl is a unique and gifted Renaissance man—not only an extremely gifted surgeon but an adjunct English literature professor at a nearby prestigious university.

His specialty is reconstructive surgery and each year, he assembles a group of medical professionals and supplies, and they fly off to some third-world country for two weeks. While there, they drastically improve the quality of people's lives by surgically repairing harelips, cleft palates and an assortment of disfiguring birth defects and injuries.

Karl often spends his own money to subsidize this venture, yet never allows the public to know of his many good deeds. He shuns publicity touting his accomplishments.

Karl feels that his contribution to the impoverished, indigent, disfigured and often shunned of the world is too minute to be mentioned. He is my hero in many ways.

Karl, a gentle giant, is an excellent amateur chef. He had always wanted to experience working in a restaurant, to see if he had what it took to be a chef. One Thursday evening, I granted his wish and put him to work on the line. He was like a hungry kid in a candy shop. What a hoot!

I was a little concerned about the safety of his hands and wanted to put him somewhere safe and far away from knives; however, he would not hear of it. The kitchen actually got a kick out of his presence and everyone had a positive experience.

After I sold the restaurant, Karl complained to me about how much he missed the Bolognese and dining at Sentimento, and of course, the fact that he could no longer work the line there. Every time I make Bolognese, I deliver a container to his office and have offered to make a barter arrangement with him. I'll keep him supplied with Bolognese for life if he keeps me supplied with Botox for life.

We are still negotiating the terms.

Chapter 25

Forget San Francisco! I Left My Heart in Summit!

When I began looking for the perfect location for my dream restaurant, Summit is where I began my quest. It had the perfect demographics for what I was trying to accomplish.

Summit is a wonderful, unique community located in northern New Jersey. It is nestled among the affluent towns of Chatham, Millburn, Morristown, Madison and Short Hills. The homes are distinctive and diverse in style, on streets that are tree-lined, with ancient deciduous greenery. Driving through the residential area of Summit, you are immediately aware that you are in an affluent and extremely genteel community. The massive, manicured lawns, along with the beautiful landscaping, are a remarkable sight—gorgeous, yet understated.

Before I decided on Summit for the location of Sentimento, I did extensive homework, researching and studying the demographics available to me.

One of the most important requirements was that it was only a fifteen-minute drive to my home—imperative when your workday ends at one or two o'clock in the morning. It is centrally located bordered by Route 24 and I-78, and only a few minutes from the Garden State Parkway and Route 22.

Summit has approximately twenty thousand residents and a beautiful train station, and is located only a short thirty minutes from New York City via New Jersey Transit's midtown direct train from Penn Station. Most important of all of its many positive qualities was the fact that it possesses a busy and prominent downtown area. The city of Summit has an incredible and eclectic array of beautiful shops, restaurants, art galleries and specialty stores. In my opinion, Sentimento was to be the perfect addition to the thriving downtonwn!

They have several impressive art galleries, antique dealers and fabulous gift shops, all virtually guaranteeing a stream of potentially moneyed and hungry diners. In June, when the town has its famous Summit Sale Days, it draws customers from all over the surrounding area and New York City.

There are loads of great restaurants and beautiful wine shops to accommodate the many BYOB dining establishments. Summit, in many ways, is unique, not because of its geographical location, but because of its residents and merchants. It is an extremely friendly, considerate and philanthropic community. Summit not only encompasses a successful downtown; it also has a strong cultural atmosphere.

Summit is a dream come true for a restaurant or business. They still have a Halloween parade and a Memorial Day parade, breakfast with Santa and other family-oriented activities. It is known for its "red hot" downtown and has many events throughout the year that attract tourists, which in turn keeps businesses booming.

I was welcomed into the business community immediately and was overwhelmed by many of the merchants' generosity of spirit; however, the other restaurants in town did not exactly welcome me with open arms. The boutique owners all asked for my business cards to leave at their shops, to distribute to their customers; the wine shops offered to keep in stock any wines we required for cooking.

There was even a liquor store that was willing to deliver wine to our customers while they dined with us. Every night, I would watch with wonder while the drunken deliveryman would ride his bike up and down the street, lit cigarette balanced on his bottom lip as he delivered wine to the various BYOB establishments.

When Overlook Hospital in Summit celebrated their centennial anniversary, I was proud to attend their gala celebration, along with twelve hundred others. It was so wonderful to see so many former customers and old friends.

Although I do not miss the daily aggravation and drama that goes hand in hand with operating a restaurant, I must admit that I miss the fantastic people of Summit and all my wonderful former customers. They were all an important part of my life for several years, and in many ways, became an extended family of sorts.

My advice is run, don't walk, to downtown Summit and experience the ambiance! Visit the many unique boutiques specializing in everything from couture baby clothes and furniture to pampered pet accessories. If you have the opportunity, visit Summit and see for yourself. Treat yourself to an Italian roast coffee or a latte; browse the Summit Antiques Center; have a cocktail at one of the many venues; and have dinner at one of the many fabulous dining establishments. Browse and window shop along Springfield Avenue and if the weather is right, dine *al fresco* at any of the many dining venues.

Experience the magic that is Summit!

Chapter 26

Celebrities, Rumors and the Sale

Over the years we had many famous—and in some cases infamous—celebrity customers dine in our restaurant. We enjoyed serving rock stars, actors, Court TV celebrities, famous lawyers, renowned forensic pathologists, politicians, TV news anchors and numerous sports figures.

In my opinion, the interactions I experienced with these people were wonderful. The more accomplished and renowned the individual, in general, the nicer they were. We also served quite a few celebrities and high-profile individuals who later became convicted felons, their transgressions often creating compelling newspaper articles. We ran the gamut of serving fascinating individuals from a gastronomy maven later convicted of embezzlement to millionaires convicted of everything from income tax evasion and blackmail to multiple deeds of avarice and fraud.

While I owned Sentimento, I never really thought of myself as being in the public eye, although obviously, I was. I do not view myself as a philistine and do not indulge in self-aggrandizement; however, I became the topic of numerous rumors and gossip during the Sentimento years.

The loquacious and viciousness of the rumors were extremely disconcerting. One of the more popular tales was that Vincent and I were getting divorced and were closing the restaurant due to a contentious and egregious separation and a bitter arbitration settlement dispute. I sold Sentimento over a year ago and the rumors concerning divorce allegations continue to circulate.

I am still shocked by the way those who had known us for many years would actually believe some of these fictitious stories. I was at a wedding last year, escorted by

Vincent, when an old friend sitting next to me leaned over and whispered, "Word on the street is that you sold out because of a nasty divorce. Sorry to hear it."

I could not believe that someone who I considered a friend would say that to me, especially in such an arrogant and obnoxious manner, and at a social occasion. I thought for a second and then replied, "Oh, really? What street was that?"

His reply was a snort and a nod before he stated, "Everyone knows you're here tonight for 'show and tell' purposes."

"I can't believe you just said that to me. Who is 'everyone'? Haven't you noticed who is sitting to my left? If we were in the midst of a hostile divorce, do you actually think we would be sitting here?"

He gave me a smug smirk and said, "I'm just repeating what I've been told. I have a reliable source."

"You know, they call that type of garrulous talk 'gossip' for a reason. I would really like to know the name of the street this talk is coming from, since you stated 'word on the street.' Where did you hear this and who is this reliable source?"

He merely leaned back in his chair and in a haughty and supercilious tone, said, "Why don't you just admit it and give up the façade? Everyone knows Vinnie moved out of your house."

At this juncture in the conversation, I decided to include Vincent. I tugged on his sleeve and said, "Vincent, I think Joel has something to ask you."

Since Vinnie was very unaware of the conversation that had just transpired, he leaned over with a big smile and said, "What's up?"

Joel's portly face turned scarlet in hue as he cleared his throat and held up an index finger to indicate that we should "wait a second," and he began a fake cough and reached for a glass of water. He continued his falsetto coughing fit and excused himself as he headed toward the bar. Vinnie resumed his chat with the fellow sitting on his left; he was clueless concerning Joel's offensive conversation.

The most recent story had Vince abandoning our family and me for a woman in her twenties. A few months ago, while we were out to dinner with close friends, my friend Jean related a recent conversation she had with a mutual acquaintance of ours. Jean had bumped into this woman at the Short Hills Mall and stopped to chat briefly. Jean innocently inquired, "How have you been?"

The woman blurted out that her husband had left her for another woman! She dramatically stated that she was in the midst of a nasty divorce, including far more information than my pal Jean required.

Jean, a compassionate woman, was standing there, sympathetically listening to this woman's tale of woe, when Fay, the shrewish bitch, stated, "Well, if you want to know what it's like, just ask your friend, Ivy. I heard the divorce is about to be finalized. In fact, I was going to call you for Vinnie's new phone number. I know he's tight with Jack. I'm not interested, but I have a friend who would be perfect for him. Ya think he might be interested? She has a mansion on the Navesink and a gorgeous condo on the water in Boca, and an apartment in New York."

My friend Jean, a beautiful and confident woman, smiled at her and said, "Your information source is incorrect. They are not separated, divorced or about to be. In fact, they are in St. Martin right now—together! We are going to dinner with them next Saturday night."

"I know you've always been loyal to Ivy, but I got my four-one-one from a very reliable source," said Fay. "I heard it by the pool at the Breakers when I was visiting my friend, Colleen, in Palm Beach. There were two women discussing it. Women we both know. I know it's true. Besides, she deserved it. She was always pretending to be so happy and acted so superior, like they were such a loving couple. It was all just bullshit!"

At this point, Jean had had enough of the virulent Fay and her false allegations, and verbally tore Fay a new orifice. Fay never repeated the story again…at least as far as we know.

I think what infuriated me the most after hearing Jean relate the story was that even at the height of the gossip, no one ever called me for a date!

Over the years, I dealt with ubiquitous rumors, a dipsomaniacal staff that could drive one to distraction, and a psychotic executive chef who clearly possessed contradictory aspirations from mine. I employed an interesting array of outrageous and often unstable employees over the years that provided me with constant entertainment and aggravation.

I tolerated Christopher's absurd behavior, temper tantrums and his tendency to put a certain brand of eye drops in my food when he was really pissed off at me; adding this unwanted ingredient to my dinner would guarantee an outburst of diarrhea accompanied by severe cramps.

I dealt with servers who often appeared to be devoid of intellect and behaved in a devious manner. They not only stole steaks from me but also furnished their apartments with full sets of Sentimento crystal glasses, silverware and china—yet would have the nerve to call us when they were arrested and would actually have the gall to expect me to bail them out of jail.

Many of my employees thought we were "The Bank of Zingara," and constantly borrowed money from us when they became embroiled in financial struggles, which was quite frequently. I have to state that in all the years we operated the restaurant and lent money to our employees, there was only one who did not repay the loan.

His name was Carlito and he was a runner/busboy. He was an excellent employee, although he was often victimized by Christopher and on two occasions, actually wept with frustration. Vincent gave him an advance on his salary of three hundred dollars the week before we sold Sentimento. Unfortunately, Vincent forgot to later deduct it from Carlito's final paycheck.

We contacted him numerous times in an effort to collect the debt and eventually just mentally wrote it off. Last fall, we were having dinner with friends at a local restaurant when Vince received a text message that required an immediate response. It was an important business matter, so he excused himself in order to walk outside, so he could return the call without disturbing anyone.

As he exited the bar area, he heard someone yelling, "Mr. Vincent, Mr. Vincent!"

Vince turned to see Carlito running to greet him. Carlito said, "Is Ivy here? I miss her so much. She was so nice to me. I still have the coat she gave me when I didn't got one. My cousin Alfredo still has the coat she give him. I no miss Christopher but I miss you guys!"

Vincent replied, "Ivy is in the dining room. She's sitting with the Ostrowskys, the couple who always wanted to sit outside at table forty-one, or at table thirty inside. Do you remember them?"

Carlito nodded emphatically, indicating that he indeed recalled Dr. and Mrs. Ostrowsky. He excitedly said, "I go see Miss Ivy now and surprise her!"

At this point, Vincent warned him that I might not be very friendly since he had never repaid the three hundred dollars we loaned him. Obviously, Carlito decided to disregard the advice and dashed into the dining room looking for me.

While Vincent was MIA making his phone call, I was engrossed in a conversation with Joyce and Nat, our dining companions. That is, until Carlito ran up to our table shouting, "Ivy, Ivy!"

He appeared to be genuinely thrilled to see me, which was confusing, since he owed me three hundred dollars. He hugged me and said, "I miss you guys so much! You were the nicest boss I ever have!"

I thanked him for his kind words and said I was glad to see him. I wanted to ask him for the three hundred, but I did not want to embarrass myself in front of the Ostrowskys, former customers who have become close friends over the years. I thought I might appear tacky and possibly vulgar if I were to mention the money he owed me, especially since he seemed so happy to see me.

He informed me that he was a bartender and asked us to stop by the lounge on the way out so that he could buy us a drink. I said, "Sure. I'll tell Vincent you're working here and we'll see you on the way out."

"Oh, I already see Vincent. That how I know you here."

I thought that if Vincent already saw him, maybe he had asked for the money or Carlito had made an arrangement with him to repay the three hundred dollars. As soon as Carlito left, I could no longer control myself. I stated in a mumbled growl to Joyce and Nat, "He owes me three hundred dollars!"

When Vincent returned to the table, he asked, "Did Carlito come over to the table?"

I nodded and he said, "I warned him you might not be thrilled to see him since he never paid us back."

Joyce and Nat started laughing and Nat said, "As soon as he walked away Ivy said, 'He owes me three hundred dollars!'"

He still owes me three hundred dollars.

I worked very diligently during my Sentimento years to operate an efficient and successful business. I attempted to guarantee a fantastic dining experience while sitting on ergonomically friendly chairs in a romantic atmosphere accompanied by efficient, competent and amicable servers who were not intrusive.

The key to a successful restaurant is not merely an excellent chef and a fabulous location; *au contraire*, it also requires dedication, hard work, long and often grueling hours and the ability to effectively deal with the daily exigent circumstances that constantly arise.

It was often a conundrum how to efficiently create a "cease fire" between Christopher and the servers during the dinner rush, or how to quell an extremely bombastic diner who was disturbing the others around him. You do your best to prevail.

I often miss the cacophonous cackle emanating from the dining room, the wonderful customers I was fortunate to meet, the Sentimento dogs, the gourmands and the numerous glamazons who decorated the restaurant nightly.

When I begin to feel sentimental about Sentimento, I try to remember the fist fights in the kitchen. During one such altercation between a line cook and a waiter, the only person injured was me! I try to recall the employees who stole, lied and spied, and the ubiquitous gossip about us.

It is a virtual certainty that global commerce was not impacted by the sale of Sentimento; however, the way I carried on, one would think it was. Once Vincent received that final offer, he was adamant that I agree to sell. I was not ready to, but Vincent wanted our lives back. The restaurant had taken over my life and in many ways, *was* my life.

I felt pressured by Vincent and powerless due to the gossip mongers and their circulating stories. Our employees were aware of the rumors and feared for the security of their positions and continued employment. I still feel as though I should have had more options. I wanted to have the prerogative to sell it on my terms when and if I chose to; but that just wasn't the case.

The end result was that Vincent, as much as I hate to admit it, was right. It turned out to be the perfect time to sell and the prospective buyer's bid was an extremely enticing offer. We accepted it!

Someone once told me that every ending was just another way of saying that there was a new beginning just around the corner. I did not believe it then, but I think I can accept it now. I am ready, willing and able to enjoy my "new beginning" as the next chapter of my life unfolds.

The next time you are dining out at a favorite restaurant, I would like to request that you pause for a moment, glance around the dining room and try to imagine the drama that might be going on behind the clatter of the closed kitchen doors.

The ultimate and final truth is this: I would not have missed one second of my Sentimento adventure.

BON APPETIT!
Ciao!